Participation in Christ

COLUMBIA SERIES IN REFORMED THEOLOGY

The Columbia Series in Reformed Theology represents a joint commitment of Columbia Theological Seminary and Westminster John Knox Press to provide theological resources for the church today.

The Reformed tradition has always sought to discern what the living God revealed in Scripture is saying and doing in every new time and situation. Volumes in this series examine significant individuals, events, and issues in the development of this tradition and explore their implications for contemporary Christian faith and life.

This series is addressed to scholars, pastors, and laypersons. The Editorial Board hopes that these volumes will contribute to the continuing reformation of the church.

Columbia Theological Seminary wishes to express its appreciation to the following churches for supporting this joint publishing venture:

Central Presbyterian Church, Atlanta, Georgia
First Presbyterian Church, Franklin, Tennessee
First Presbyterian Church, Nashville, Tennessee
First Presbyterian Church, Quincy, Florida
First Presbyterian Church, Spartanburg, South Carolina
First Presbyterian Church, Tupelo, Mississippi
North Avenue Presbyterian Church, Atlanta, Georgia
Riverside Presbyterian Church, Jacksonville, Florida
Roswell Presbyterian Church, Roswell, Georgia
South Highland Presbyterian Church, Birmingham, Alabama
Spring Hill Presbyterian Church, Mobile, Alabama
St. Simons Island Presbyterian Church, St. Simons Island, Georgia
St. Stephen Presbyterian Church, Fort Worth, Texas
Trinity Presbyterian Church, Atlanta, Georgia
University Presbyterian Church, Chapel Hill, North Carolina

COLUMBIA SERIES IN REFORMED THEOLOGY

Participation in Christ

An Entry into Karl Barth's Church Dogmatics

ADAM NEDER

 WESTMINSTER
JOHN KNOX PRESS
LOUISVILLE · KENTUCKY

First edition
Westminster John Knox Press
Louisville, Kentucky

09 10 11 12 13 14 15 16 17 18—10 9 8 7 6 5 4 3 2 1

Book and cover design by Drew Stevens

Library of Congress Cataloging-in-Publication Data

Neder, Adam.
  Participation in Christ : an entry into Karl Barth's Church dogmatics / Adam Neder.—1st ed.
      p. cm.—(Columbia series in Reformed theology)
  Includes bibliographical references (p.   ) and index.
  ISBN 978-0-664-23460-7 (alk. paper)
  1. Barth, Karl, 1886–1968. Kirchliche Dogmatik.   2. Jesus Christ—Person and offices.
3. Participation.   I. Title.
  BT205.H45   2009
  232.092—dc22

                                                                                    2009001898

CONTENTS

ACKNOWLEDGMENTS

I would like to express my gratitude to a number of people who have contributed significantly to the publication of this book. If I were to begin listing all that Dr. Bruce McCormack has taught me and done for me, both personally and professionally, over the years that I have known him, this would have to become the first chapter of the book. So with deep respect and undisguised affection, I will simply thank him for the whole lot of it. While I did not officially take a course from Dr. George Hunsinger, I nevertheless consider him my teacher. In numerous conversations and through his excellent scholarship, he has shaped my reading of Barth's *Church Dogmatics* in decisive ways. Drs. Daniel Migliore and Sang Lee offered helpful suggestions on the original version of this study. On two occasions, Drs. Stephen Crocco and Clifford Anderson allowed me generous use of the Center for Barth Studies in Speer Library at Princeton Theological Seminary. I am grateful for Whitworth University, and would like to thank my colleagues, students, and our president, Dr. William P. Robinson, for their encouragement. Dr. Donald McKim of Westminster John Knox Press has guided me through the publication process with unusual kindness, competence, and wisdom. I want to thank him and the CSRT board for their generous affirmation of my work, as well as for their helpful suggestions. For the last decade, Christian Andrews, a person of extraordinary theological and pastoral gifts, has been an invaluable friend and indispensible conversation partner. Dr. Charles, Susan, Joshua, and Luke Neder, and William and Connelly Ensign have supported and encouraged me in countless ways.

The best part of my life is living with my wife, Janet, and our daughters Mary and Claire. "Do nothing from selfish ambition or conceit, but in humility regard others as better than yourselves. Let each of you look not to your own interests, but to the interests of others" (Phil. 2:3–4). Janet embodies this attitude more fully than anyone else I know. In deepest appreciation of her love, friendship, and Christian witness, I dedicate this book to her.

ABBREVIATIONS

CD Barth, Karl. *Church Dogmatics*. 4 vols. in 13 parts. Edinburgh: T&T Clark, 1956–69.

KD Barth, Karl. *Die kirkliche Dogmatik*. 4 vols. in 13 parts. Munich: Chr. Kaiser, 1932, and Zurich: TVZ, 1938–65.

If the true being of the Christian consists in the life of Christ in him and his life in Christ, then it follows that the principle which controls Christian existence, provisionally formulated, consists in the community of action, determined by the order of the relationship between Christ and the Christian. We have in view the divine-human action in divine-human sovereignty when we speak of the being and life of Christ, and human action in human freedom when we speak of the being and life of the Christian. Christ is engaged in a work, and in perfect fellowship with Him so too is the Christian called by Him. The latter works, but he does so in perfect fellowship with the working of Christ. Everything else which takes place in this relationship, and especially the giving of Christ and the receiving of the Christian, takes place relatively to this community of action, within the context and in furtherance and consequence of it. And since the fellowship as a fellowship of action takes place in this definite and irreversible order, the action, work and activity of Christ unconditionally precedes that of the man called by Him, the Christian, and that of the latter must follow. Their fellowship of life thus finds realization as a differentiated fellowship of action in which Christ is always superior and the Christian subordinate. Hence the principle controlling Christian existence, which is our specific concern, will always necessarily result from the fact that the Christian, as he lives in Christ and Christ in him, exists in this fellowship of action and its order. Whatever else may distinguish it, it is to be understood primarily and decisively from this standpoint.

Karl Barth, *Church Dogmatics* IV/3.2

INTRODUCTION

Legend has it that after falling asleep in one of Karl Barth's seminars, a student was awoken by the sound of his professor's voice. "Please answer the question for us." Without missing a beat, the student responded, "Jesus Christ." Barth's reply: "Exactly right!" True or not, the story points to the taproot of Barth's theology: the confession that God's gracious action toward the world is concentrated "in Christ," who is both the savior of the world and its salvation, the giver of grace and grace itself. Not since the apostle Paul has one phrase so dominated a theologian's work. According to Barth, revelation, election, creation, reconciliation, and redemption all take place "in Christ," and their meaning and content may be rightly apprehended only in him.[1] In fact, the very being of humanity itself is objectively included in the being of Jesus Christ, and is likewise subjectively (i.e., by individual people) realized in him. In these acts of inclusion and realization, the creature is incorporated into a depth of fellowship that is nothing less than participation in the being of God. Statements such as these are at the heart of Barth's theology. Yet they cry out for explanation.

How can Jesus Christ be both the giver of grace and grace itself? The giver of grace surely, but grace itself? Or what does it mean to say that the being of humanity is objectively included in the being of Jesus Christ? How, precisely, should this statement be understood? And what does it mean to say that human being is subjectively realized in Christ? How can the being of humanity be both objectively included in Christ and subjectively realized in him? Surely "in Christ" means something different when referring to objective inclusion than when referring to subjective realization, but what exactly is the difference? And participation in Christ as participation in the being of God? Does Barth not go out of his way to reject deification repeatedly in every volume of the *Church Dogmatics*? If so, then how can fellowship with God be a form of participation in God? Barth certainly never let go of his commitment to the ineradicable distinction between the Creator and his creatures. But how does this commitment square with his assertion that salvation means participation in God's being? The deeper one delves into Barth's theology, the more such questions abound.

METHOD AND GOALS

This study is an attempt to answer these and related questions as precisely as possible through a careful examination of Barth's understanding of participation in Christ as it appears in relevant sections of the *Church Dogmatics*.[2] Barth utilizes Calvin's concept of *participatio Christi* in his treatment of sanctification in *CD* IV/2, but that discussion does not arise out of thin air and is by no means a full expression of Barth's thought on the matter.[3] Already in the first volume of the *Church Dogmatics*, Barth interacts with Augustine, Luther, and Calvin on the issue of the *unio hominis cum Christo* [4]— the "mutual indwelling that occurs between the Word and human beings" (*Beieinanderseins des Wortes und eines Menschen*)[5]—and he enhances and develops his description of the nature of divine-human union in the second, third, and fourth volumes of that work. Barth's treatment of participation in Christ as he sets it forth in the context of the doctrine of sanctification in the fourth volume of the *Church Dogmatics* is an elaboration of an idea that was already present in the first volume.[6] Moreover, far from being a minor aspect of his thought, this theme belongs to the fundamental core of Barth's theology, is present in one way or another in virtually every part of the *Church Dogmatics*, and understanding it is essential for understanding the work as a whole.

Thus, this study has three goals—two primary and one secondary. First, I will elucidate and analyze Barth's understanding of participation in Christ as it unfolds through the *Church Dogmatics*. Second, I will show that this theme is not a late development in Barth's thought, but is present at the outset of the *Church Dogmatics* and functions importantly throughout the work as a whole. Finally, an indirect goal of the study is that it should serve as a somewhat unconventional introduction to a number of the major themes of the *Church Dogmatics* as a whole.

Yet anyone even casually acquainted with the *Church Dogmatics* knows that its complexity and sheer length present massive interpretive challenges. Moreover, those challenges are even greater than they would be if I were attempting to trace a theme farther removed from the nucleus of the *Church Dogmatics*. Thus the question arises as to whether or not it is even possible to write on such a fundamental and pervasive theme in the *Church Dogmatics* so as to illuminate rather than obscure it, and indeed to do so without sacrificing comprehensiveness, accuracy, or depth.[7]

I am, of course, convinced that it is possible, and that the best way to do so is to read the *Church Dogmatics* as a whole and then to set textual parameters within which one patiently interacts with Barth's arguments as they unfold within a given section. The first step, admittedly daunting, is one that few attempt, including many who write on Barth's theology, yet its payoff is incalculable, for it affords the reader a grasp of the whole within which to interpret any given part. Carefully following Barth's argument within a given section—rather than constructing an interpretive thesis and then supporting it with proof texts culled from various places throughout the *Church Dogmatics*—yields a richer and more accurate interpretation. It is much easier to flatly misunderstand or subtly misrepresent Barth's theology if one ignores those aspects of it which do not support the interpretation being advanced.

Yet given the sheer length of the *Church Dogmatics*, how does one determine the most relevant sections to examine without being arbitrary and without ignoring important material? This is a difficult question to answer. The nature of the method that I have chosen leaves the investigation open to the potential criticism that I have failed to treat important materials. In anticipation of this criticism, as well as a few others, let me point out five things.

First, the *Church Dogmatics* is comprised of over nine thousand densely argued pages, and therefore anyone who chooses to interpret it faces the problem of which sections to treat, no matter which method she uses. Second, if the theme of participation in Christ is developed in important ways within the sections that I have chosen to analyze, then my selection of those sections would be warranted. Third, with every foray into new dogmatic territory, Barth found it necessary to recapitulate a great deal of the preceding material. This aspect of Barth's theology is well known and best described by Barth himself: "In theological science, continuation always means 'beginning once again at the beginning.'"[8] Barth does not simply offer a definitive treatment of an issue never again to return to it, but continually revisits all the major dogmatic themes from a new perspective as he deals directly with each one. The *Church Dogmatics* proceeds less in the form of straightforward sequential argument than as a slowly moving gradual accumulation of elaborations and recapitulations on dogmatic themes; it is more like an avalanche than an arrow. Since this is the case, the chance of completely missing some key ingredient of his overall teaching concerning participation in Christ is reduced. Fourth, I examine sections from every volume of the *Church Dogmatics*. This does not guarantee that I have treated every important issue related to participation in Christ, but it certainly increases the likelihood that I have. Finally, one might argue that while the method I have chosen is a valid one, employing it within a narrower range would have been preferable. Would it not have been better, for example, to examine the theme of participation in Christ strictly within the volume on reconciliation? The subject certainly figures significantly enough in that volume to justify such an approach. Yet the choice to begin treatment of the material in the fourth volume would be inferior to the method that I have chosen, for one simple reason: the theme of participation in Christ is significantly present in all four volumes of the *Church Dogmatics*. In fact, an important aspect of this study is to show that such is the case. Of course, it would be an equally serious mistake to fail to allow the fourth volume to speak in its own voice, to force the texts to say something that one expects to hear rather than to struggle to listen to what they actually say. But one need not make that mistake. The first three volumes lead one to expect Barth to handle participation in Christ in the fourth volume in ways that, as it turns out, he does in fact handle it. But is that so surprising? While Barth doesn't simply repeat conclusions already established, he does presuppose and build upon them, and the end result is a description of participation in Christ that is marked by a deep continuity throughout the *Church Dogmatics*.

OVERVIEW OF THE STUDY

In the first three chapters, I examine sections from the first three volumes of the *Church Dogmatics* respectively. In chapters 4 and 5, I treat materials from the fourth volume. Chapter 1 examines Barth's doctrine of revelation, paying special attention to the nature of the union that occurs in revelation between the Word of God and human beings. Barth depicts this as a union in active distinction, which occurs in the communion of free divine lordship and correspondingly free human obedience. Revelation is a dynamic event of mutual indwelling between the Word of God and those who receive the Word. Union with Christ *happens* in revelation. In chapter 2, I show that as election is a decision in which God determines his own being, so too is human being enacted in obedient response to this decision. Through his life of obedience *for* humanity, Jesus Christ objectively establishes the being and identity *of* humanity. Analogously, subjective participation in Christ occurs in the event of obedience, in which human beings embrace and enact their being as Jesus Christ has objectively defined it for them. God shares himself with human beings by becoming their gracious Lord. Human beings participate in God by becoming his grateful disciples. Thus, participation in Christ takes both an objective and a subjective form, the former being teleologically directed to the latter and thereby guaranteeing its genuine occurrence. Jesus Christ's life history, grounded in election, constitutes the covenant of grace, and therefore participation in Christ is participation in the covenant. Chapter 3 examines the covenantal-historical anthropology that flows from Barth's doctrine of election. Subjective participation in Christ is a history in which creatures transcend their limits, not by becoming divine, but by becoming genuinely human. I show that Barth grounds his understanding of subjective participation in Christ in his "historical" construal of the hypostatic union. In chapter 4, I argue that the opening section of the doctrine of reconciliation should be understood as an extended ontological preface to the volume as a whole. I then explain Barth's Christological conception of grace and elucidate his teaching concerning the three aspects of the one grace of Jesus Christ (justification, sanctification, and calling), which together constitute the objective being of humanity and call forth the corresponding threefold response (faith, love, and hope) in which this being is subjectively realized. The fifth chapter explores the covenantal Christology that opens the second part-volume of the doctrine of reconciliation, and shows that rightly interpreting it is the key to rightly interpreting Barth's understanding of participation in Christ. After commenting on Barth's doctrine of sanctification, I treat his doctrine of vocation as it appears in the third part-volume of the doctrine of reconciliation. This final section recapitulates and strengthens much of the argument of the study as a whole. In the Conclusion, I pursue some critical questions about Barth's position and then explore Barth's interesting relationship to Orthodox understandings of salvation as *theosis*.

1

THE *EVENT* OF UNION WITH CHRIST

Barth's conception of dogmatics is grounded in his understanding of revelation, which governs his doctrine of participation in Christ as he articulates it in *CD* I/1. As an ecclesial activity, dogmatics proceeds from the Word of God and remains ever and solely accountable to it. Its task is free speech in obedient response to God's speech, which is its sole criterion. Responsible to revelation alone, Christian theology hears and bears witness to the Word of God. Therefore, it does not attempt to justify itself through appeals to authorities external to revelation. Dogmatics is possible for one reason alone: because of the speaking and hearing of God's Word. Thus, all attempts to ground dogmatics in anything other than the Word of God are in fact betrayals of revelation, since there is, by definition, no higher court of appeals on the basis of which revelation and theological speech about revelation might be justified. Genuine knowledge of God and speech about him are possible and actual because God makes them so. Christian theology presupposes this fact and makes no attempt to establish it. Prolegomena, therefore, is internal to dogmatics.

According to Barth, revelation is not merely the offering and acquisition of information. It is rational, to be sure, since it is the divine reason communicating with human reason. But since it is *Dei loquentis persona*, it is an event in which God establishes an orderly fellowship between himself and human beings. "God's Word means that God speaks,"[1] and since it is God who speaks, to hear his Word is not simply to become aware of him, but to obediently acknowledge him as Lord. Thus revelation is inseparable from reconciliation. Moreover, knowledge of God is communion with God in Jesus Christ by the power of the Holy Spirit, and as such involves the death and resurrection of the human knower. To know God is to be joined to him in faith and obedience. The connection with participation in Christ is clear: "As God's Word is spoken to man, it is in him and he is in the Word."[2] Barth refers to this union as a "mutual indwelling [*Beieinanderseins*] of the Word and man."[3] In this chapter, I will examine Barth's description of this event in paragraphs five and six of *CD* I/1, in which he takes up the questions of the nature and knowability of God's Word respectively.

"THE NATURE OF THE WORD OF GOD" (*CD* § 5)

Union without Synthesis

Paragraph five opens with a small-print section in which Barth conceded that the doctrine of the Word of God set forth in his *Christliche Dogmatik im Entwurf* (1927) stood in need of revision.[4] In that work, Barth had mistakenly given the impression that "an anthropology, albeit a Church anthropology, was being advanced as the supposed basis on which we know decisive statements about the Word of God."[5] While he denied that his more precise statements about the Word of God were actually derived from that source, Barth admitted that he "proceeded as though they could and should be."[6] In the *Church Dogmatics*, Barth sought to remedy this mistake by framing the discussion around a single crucial question: Does God's Word ever become part of human existence? If it does, then human existence may properly serve as a source and support for dogmatic statements about the Word of God. In Barth's view, both liberal Protestant and Roman Catholic dogmatics, each in its own way, proceed along that route. Barth's own answer to the question is unmistakable: "If there is one thing the Word of God certainly is not, it is not a predicate of man, even of the man who receives it, and therefore not of the man who speaks, hears and knows it in the sphere of the Church."[7]

Barth's position is both clear and radical. Since God's Word is *God's* Word, it remains indissolubly distinct from anything creaturely even as it is spoken. To assert otherwise would constitute a denial of God's freedom and lordship through a confusion of nature and grace. God's Word is always accompanied by "a physical event," since it is directed to human beings, but it is not thereby transformed into something natural.[8] God's Word is God's personal speech, not an object which can be separated from God and subsequently quantified and assessed.

This line of argument is an attempt to provide a description of revelation that coheres with what Barth thinks actually happens when God speaks. And what happens is an event of divine lordship. The content of the Word of God is a *concretissimum*: "God always has something specific to say to each man, something that applies to him and to him alone,"[9] and that which God says "aims at us and smites us in our existence."[10] As both grace and judgment, the Word of God "creates not only a new light and therewith a new situation, but also with the new situation a new man who did not exist before but who exists now."[11] God renews the broken relationship between himself and his creatures by speaking to them as their Creator and Lord. His speech is his "ruling action," and therefore when he speaks, "we come under a lordship."[12] Jesus Christ creates disciples as he becomes Lord of their existence, not as he becomes part of their existence.

He unites himself with them, but within this union, he never becomes confused with them.

For our purposes, it is important to specify the exact concern motivating Barth's rejection of the idea that God's Word becomes a predicate of human being. His position is not merely negative. In fact, he insists on the distinction between God and human creatures as a way of *affirming* the reality of their union with one another. Knowledge of God occurs as an event of divine-human union. But Barth is convinced that in order to truly affirm this union, he must describe it in a manner appropriate to the identities of its participants. The nature of the union itself is what rules out the possibility that the Word of God can become a predicate of human existence. Since Jesus Christ freely and graciously establishes the union and always remains Lord of it, no such synthesis could possibly take place, because if it did Jesus Christ would cease to be the Lord that he is. Yet union with Christ *can* occur precisely because it takes place as an event of divine lordship and human obedience.

Veiling and Unveiling

Having reached this point in his argument, Barth proceeds to take up the issue with which I opened this chapter. If the object of theology, the Word of God, is never at the disposal and command of the theologian, then how can we show that our statements about God's Word are really statements about God's Word? Barth refuses to shy away from the answer implied in his doctrine of revelation: Christian theology *cannot* prove that it is actually speaking about the Word of God. "Only the Logos of God Himself can provide the proof that we are really talking about Him when we are allegedly doing so."[13] The Word of God is objective, but it is also *sui generis*, and therefore it cannot be demarcated from other objects. If we could point to God's Word and distinguish it from other words, then we would have seized control of it and reversed our relationship to it. We would have become its masters, and "the object of all pride in theology is to think one can really do this."[14] Nevertheless, while we cannot distinguish God's Word, God's Word distinguishes itself, and this self-distinguishing belongs to its mystery.

Relying heavily on Luther, Barth argues that God mysteriously reveals himself in the midst of concealment, unveiling himself through the veil of a creaturely form. The Word of God always exists in this secularity. God speaks to human beings in a creaturely form, and therefore in a form that contradicts his Word, not only because that form is creaturely, but also because it belongs to a fallen cosmos. As God reveals himself, he never becomes directly identical with the medium through which he reveals himself. In other words, he does not transform himself into something creaturely in order to reveal himself, but reveals himself through creaturely media while remaining absolutely distinct from those media. Every experience of God's Word is mediated. Individuals may desire an unmediated face-to-face encounter with God. They may search for it and even claim to have experienced it. But if it were actually to happen, if God were to reveal himself directly to sinful human beings apart from the veil of creaturely media, there could be only one result: the total annihilation of the sinner.

> It is good for us that God acts as He does and it could only be fatal for us if He did not, if He were manifest to us in the way we think right, directly or without veil, without secularity or only in the innocuous secularity that can be pierced by the *analogia entis*. It would not be love and mercy but *the end of us and all things*.[15]

This leads Barth to conclude that faith, the manner in which revelation is received, always remains under God's control and is never given to the recipient as a possession. It is truly given, and so it will take the form of thoughts, words, experiences, etc., but these remain intrinsically unaltered even as they bear the content of revelation. Faith is a miracle, and its recipients remain ever incapable of demonstrating the connections between the veil of thoughts, words, and experiences in which revelation is received and the God who unveils himself through them. "Considered in and of itself," Barth writes, "our thinking is irrefutably non-Christian."[16] In other words, the creaturely forms in which God is received must themselves be justified and sanctified. To elevate our thoughts and experience to the status of direct witnesses to God's presence would be to deny the indirectness of revelation, and "to want to know God directly means righteousness by works."[17] Barth insists that "the search for a receptacle of human experience, attitude and teaching which would be undoubtedly and unequivocally the receptacle of the divine content . . . is pointless."[18] Therefore he concludes that:

> faith is acknowledgment (*Anerkennung*) of our limit (*Grenze*) and acknowledgment of the mystery of God's Word, acknowledgment of the fact that our hearing is bound to God Himself, who now leads us through form to content and now from content back to form [*der uns je durch die Gestalt zum Gehalt und durch den Gehalt zurück zur Gestalt*], and either way to Himself, not giving Himself in either case into our hands but keeping us in His hands.[19]

Thus, Barth stresses the limits, the boundaries of revelation, the distinction between God and the creature within this event. His point is clear and unequivocal: to refuse to admit this limit is to deny both faith and its object. But Barth is not intent on keeping God and human beings forever separate.

He has no interest in erecting an ineradicable wall between God and the creature, one that God shouts over, so to speak, but never really crosses. In fact, all of Barth's emphasis on the indirectness of the knowledge of faith, the veiling of revelation in creaturely forms, and the hiddenness of God, *is for the sake of God's unveiling*. The hidden God really does reveal himself, he really does unveil himself in this veiling. While Barth finds it necessary to chasten what he regards to be mistaken assumptions concerning the nature of this divine-human communion, his negative assessment of the *analogia entis* as it surfaces in Roman Catholicism, liberal Protestantism, mysticism, rationalism, existentialism, etc., is his demarcation of the limitation in which God *positively* reveals himself. Moreover, and for our purposes this is the most important point to be made clear, this unveiling is a union between God and the believer.

All of Barth's critical comments shed light on the positive affirmation that the event of revelation is an event of divine-human union. "The point of God's speech," Barth argues, "is not to occasion specific thoughts or a specific attitude, but through the clarity which God gives us, and which induces both these in us, *to bind us to Himself* [*uns an ihn selbst zu binden*]."[20] "In this divine telling there is an encounter [*Begegnung*] and fellowship [*Gemeinschaft*] between His nature and man but not an assuming of God's nature into man's knowing, only a fresh divine telling."[21] Revelation occurs in the union and communion of divine speech and human hearing, in the personal fellowship of the self-giving Lord and his grateful servants. Here in the first volume of the *Church Dogmatics*, Barth sounds a note that will recur repeatedly throughout the work. Indeed it is one of his most characteristic thoughts. All of God's gifts are forms of his self-giving, and thus revelation and reconciliation are inseparable.[22] In other words, for sinful human creatures to know God they must be reconciled to him, since God is not an abstract principle, a glorified creature, or an inert thing, but the holy and living Lord of life. According to Barth, "Revelation in fact does not differ from the person of Jesus Christ nor from the reconciliation accomplished in Him. To say revelation is to say 'The Word became flesh.'"[23]

Revelation and Reformed Christology

The previous quotation reveals the source of Barth's thinking on this matter. Barth intends to derive his doctrine of revelation exclusively from God's self-revelation in Jesus Christ. He insists on the indirectness of revelation because he is convinced that in Jesus Christ revelation is indirect rather than direct. Even with Jesus Christ, "the veil is thick."[24] "We do not have the Word of God otherwise than in the mystery of its secularity."[25] This secularity, Barth argues, is not:

a kind of fatal accident or an inconvenience which will some day be set aside either totally or at least in part. This secularity, this twofold indirectness [*doppelten Indirektheit*], is in fact an authentic and inalienable attribute of the Word of God itself. Revelation means the incarnation of the Word. But incarnation means entry into this secularity. We are in this world and are through and through secular. If God did not speak to us in secular form, He would not speak to us at all. To evade the secularity of His Word is to evade Christ.[26]

Thus, Barth's description of the indirectness of God's self-revelation through creaturely media, as well as his description of the nature of the faith by which revelation is received, applies also to the humanity of Jesus Christ. "The self-presentation of God in His Word is not direct."[27] The Word of God has assumed human flesh, but the flesh of Jesus Christ has not thereby received the Word of God as one of its predicates. It has been united with the Son of God, but it has not been transformed into something other than creaturely flesh. It has not been deified. There is, rather, an indirect relationship between the Word of God and the humanity of Jesus Christ. "Here in the *humanitas Christi* we are to seek and find everything. We seek and find this, but we seek and find; we do not see and have directly."[28] This is so not merely because as sinful and creaturely beings we lack the capacity for this perception. The *humanitas Christi* itself lacks this capacity!

This line of argument is an incorporation of Luther's theology of the cross into an essentially Reformed Christology. "The core of Luther's idea is that the *larva Dei*, the indirectness of His self-communication, is two-fold, one due to the creatureliness and the other due to the sinfulness of the creature."[29] Barth agrees with Luther that revelation is indirect, but he grounds that insight in the character of the union of divine and human natures in Jesus Christ himself—a decidedly un-Lutheran move. Whereas Luther's Christology affirmed a direct and immediate sharing of the human nature in the attributes of the divine, and in that sense is identical with the Christology of the Eastern Church, Barth's Christology takes a different route. At this stage of his development, Barth, in typically Reformed fashion, denied a direct penetration of the divine nature into the human.[30] By insisting on the inalienably secular character of the Word of God, Barth intends to cut off the source of all soteriologies which, in one way or another, affirm a cleansing or transformation of human nature through the infusion of divine grace, divine attributes, or the divine nature itself. If Jesus Christ is not divinized, then no one is. Barth makes that point as clearly as possible.

However, by working out his position in this way, Barth acknowledges the positive concern that underlies the Lutheran and Orthodox understanding of the *communicatio idiomatum*. This aspect of Barth's work has gone almost entirely unnoticed. To be sure, he has done so on the soil of a very different Christology. But Barth insists that in the event of revelation, a true union does occur. In revelation, God joins himself to us in dynamic personal fellowship. I will explore the meaning and mode of this fellowship throughout this study, but it is apparent already here in the first volume of the *Church Dogmatics* that Barth conceives of revelation as an event in which God "binds us to Himself" in the closest possible communion.

Union in Active Distinction

Before turning to paragraph six, one final observation needs to be made. Barth's affirmation of the distinction between God and human creatures within their union is a statement about the relationship between divine and human *actions* (and therefore divine and human *being*) respectively.[31] Barth does not insist on this distinction in order to affirm an abstract metaphysical doctrine of the absolute distinction between Creator and creature, but rather as a witness to the meaning of grace itself.

Grace is grace only if it is freely given and if in this giving God remains himself. More precisely, grace is the establishment and maintenance of a fellowship in which God gives himself to the creature as covenant partner, but in so doing does not give himself away. God always remains the Lord of the occurrence of this fellowship, and therefore his action to establish and maintain this fellowship always precedes and makes possible the human action of participating in it. To be God is to be the one who is always gracious; to be properly human is to be the corresponding active recipient of God's grace. This ordering of giving and receiving, preceding and following, lordship and grateful obedience, constitutes the basic difference between the parties within their fellowship. To confuse God and human beings would mean to reverse, weaken, or misunderstand the nature and ordering of these distinct actions. In Barth's view, historicism, psychologism, indeed all manifestations of the infamous *analogia entis*, are at bottom denials of God's deity through inaccurate depictions of the relationship between divine and creaturely action and therefore being. Grace is *God's* grace, and therefore must never be conceived as something distinct from God's immediate action of giving it. And the whole point is that rather than denying divine-human communion, Barth intends to highlight its intimacy and reality by describing it within a framework adequate to its participants—the utterly free and gracious Lord of the covenant and his correspondingly free and grateful servants and friends.

"THE KNOWABILITY OF THE WORD OF GOD" (*CD* § 6)

Barth is commonly criticized for debasing the gospel and evacuating human history and action of all significance by overemphasizing the objective reality of God and Jesus Christ. Faith becomes the bare cognitive awareness that something really good has already happened for the world in Jesus Christ, and human action becomes merely the mechanistic unfolding of either the fixed eternal decision of election or the crowding out of the rest of history by the execution of that eternal decision in the history of Jesus Christ. The nature of Barth's affirmation of the reality and objectivity of Jesus Christ is regarded as a denial of the reality and integrity of the created world.[32] In this section I will, among other things, begin to address the charge that Barth intellectualizes faith and knowledge of God. Later in this study, I will argue that understanding the nature of Barth's objectivism is one of the keys that unlocks his conception of participation in Christ. Yet even apart from that discussion, if one actually reads what Barth wrote on the issues of faith and knowledge of God, rather than deducing his position from what he sup- posedly thinks about the objective reality of that which was accomplished by and in Jesus Christ (especially from *CD* II/2 onward), one will be sur- prised that such a distorted perception of Barth's teaching on these matters could continue to persist in the minds of so many. Of course, misunder- standings of Barth's thought do not appear out of thin air and are usually based on one-sided readings of specific texts. In the next few paragraphs, I will briefly present some of the more well-known aspects of Barth's doctrine of the knowledge of God as he articulates it in paragraph six. I will then pre- sent important aspects of his thought that are usually overlooked and that bear significantly on the issue of the nature of divine-human union.

Familiar Themes

Perhaps the most well-known aspect of Barth's teaching concerning the knowledge of God is that it occurs "from above to below."[33] Just as the incar- nation of the Son of God is not one of the possibilities inherent within the world itself, but is rather a free decision of the triune God, so too knowledge of God is not among the world's possibilities, but comes to human beings as a free gift. "The Word of God becomes knowable by making itself known."[34] Barth builds upon the conclusions of paragraph five by arguing that during and after this event—just as before—nothing passes into human hands.

> Faith is not one of the various capacities of man, *whether native or acquired*. . . . The possibility of faith as it is given to man in the reality of faith can be understood only as one that is loaned [*geliehene*] to man by God, and loaned exclusively for use. . . . We do not understand it as a pos- sibility which is in any sense man's own.[35]

Knowledge of God is "a pure fact,"[36] wholly grounded in God, and inca- pable of being validated on any basis other than the Word. Faith looks to

Jesus Christ, not to itself, and should it decide to contemplate itself, it would find only darkness.[37] Self-understanding is significant as a source of knowledge of God only to the extent that one understands oneself as the recipient of the promises of the gospel, which are extended to every human being.[38] Here too Barth borrows from Luther—specifically his *simul iustus et peccator* doctrine. To receive God's grace does not involve becoming someone who is "new in himself, changed in the immanent constitution of his humanity . . . in a depth of his being."[39] All acknowledgment of God's Word in our experience is "unmasked and convicted by the Word of God even as it takes place, convicted not of its imperfection and inadequacy but of its *total corruption and futility*."[40]

Rather than occurring as some kind of synthesis between divine and human being and action, knowledge of God occurs as a conformity to God established by the Word of God. There is a similarity between God's grace and human faith and knowledge. The similarity is not, however, between the being of God and the being of the human creature as such, but instead between the decision of God's grace and the corresponding human decision of faith. "Not a being which the creature has in common with the Creator for all their dissimilarity, but an act that is inaccessible to any mere theory, i.e., human decision is in faith similar to the decision of God's grace for all its dissimilarity."[41] This is Barth's famous *analogia fidei*: "In faith man is in conformity to God, i.e., capable of receiving God's Word, capable of so corresponding in his own decision to the decision God has made about him in the Word that the Word is now the Word heard by him and he himself is now the man addressed by this Word."[42] Again, all of this is quite familiar. Let us now turn to the less-well-known aspects of Barth's position.

Barthian Existentialism

"The Word of God becomes knowable by making itself known."[43] That is the thesis of paragraph six. We have already seen what Barth rejects in order to safeguard this point. But his denials and affirmations both proceed from the same source—his very specific understanding of grace. Knowledge of God is a miracle of grace not only because the condition for the possibility of its occurrence lies strictly outside the creaturely sphere, but also because it occurs as a union between Christ and believers. "As God's Word is spoken to man, it is in him and he is in the Word."[44] This "mutual indwelling [*Beieinanderseins*] of the Word and man"[45] *happens* as the Word is known in faith, not as human beings receive a capacity that remains after the encounter takes place.[46] As Barth puts it, knowledge of God is conferred on human beings "by being event [*Ereignis*], so that it is man's possibility without ceasing (as such) to be wholly and utterly the possibility proper to the Word of God and to it alone."[47] Within this event, God's grace creates a new creature whose entire existence is one of free faith and gratitude. This occurs as "a radical renewal [*Erneuerung*] and therewith an obviously radical criticism of the whole of his present existence."[48]

The preceding quotation indicates the fundamental orientation of paragraph six as a whole. More than anything else, this paragraph emphasizes the categorical impact that knowledge of God has on every facet of human existence.[49] Barth existentializes the knowledge of God.[50] If the standard criticism of his theology is that he intellectualizes faith and evacuates it of its practical significance, paragraph six is the perfect counterpoint. "We know" the Word of God, Barth writes, "when we can only affirm it because we ourselves are its actualization *in our entire existence*."[51] When one considers the knowledge of God, "the decisive point materially is that it is a determination of the whole self-determining man."[52] "To have experience of God's Word is to yield to its supremacy."[53] The "Word of God comes as a summons [*Aufruf*] to [a person] and the hearing it finds in him is the right hearing of obedience [*Gehorsam*] or the wrong hearing of disobedience."[54] Notice that Barth is not merely linking knowledge and obedience, but equating them, and he does so to emphasize that knowledge of God is altogether active and existentially transformative. To know God's Word does not merely involve the acquisition of knowledge about God's Word. It includes that, of course.[55] But it goes beyond that because it is personal knowledge, and since the person known is the Lord, the relation established is a "relation of total subjection and need" (*Verhältnis des gänzlichen Unterliegenes und Bedürfens*).[56]

Moreover, this "co-existence" (*Zusammensein*) of God and human beings is not servile submission, but *free* obedience.[57]

> When acknowledgment takes place, there is a yielding of the man who acknowledges before the thing or person he acknowledges. He submits to the authority of the other. This is not in contradiction with the concept of self-determination but it does mean that the self-determination of man as such takes place at a specific point in a specific context. It has found its beginning and its basis in another higher determination. In the act of acknowledgment, the life of man, without ceasing to be the self-determining life of this man, has now its center, its whence, the meaning of its attitude. . . . The final thing to be said is that while the attitude of acknowledgment vis-a-vis God's Word is really an attitude of man, an act of his self-determination, nevertheless it is the act of that self-determination of man whose meaning and basis, whose final seriousness and true content, whose truth and reality, cannot be ascribed to man himself but only to his determination by the Word of God.[58]

Barth uses two key terms interchangeably to describe this event: conformity to God (*Gottförmig*) and correspondence (*Entsprechung*). Both are present in the following quotation: "In faith man is in conformity to God, i.e., capable of receiving God's Word, capable of so corresponding in his own decision to the decision God has made about him in the Word that the Word is now the Word heard by him and he himself is now the man addressed by this Word."[59] In this event of correspondence, God's free grace establishes and upholds human freedom. The union of the Word with those who know the Word *occurs* as these two actions—the divine determination of lordship and the human response of free faith and obedience—are united in a single event. Within this union, divine and human actions are not separated or divided from one another, and thus there is a real union, a mutual indwelling. Yet neither are they confused with one another or secretly changed into one another, as Barth repeatedly stresses with his rejection of the ideas of synthesis and cooperation and his insistence that faith and knowledge of God are miraculous in character. Mutual indwelling occurs not as the actualization of a natural human capacity, but as the liberation of human action by God's sovereign grace, which energizes human creatures to freely do that which by nature is impossible for them.

Barthian Spirituality

Before concluding this chapter, let us look at this event from two final angles. According to Barth, the content of union with Christ is not moral improvement, gradual cleansing, purification of consciousness, or inward transformation of some form or another. It is the death and resurrection of the sinner. In this encounter, a new creature appears on the scene that did not exist before the event. Thus, when Barth, against Emil Brunner, argues that the image of God in human beings has not been "destroyed apart from a few relics," but has been "totally annihilated" (*vernichtet*), his rationale stems directly from this perception.[60]

> The image of God in man of which we must speak here and which forms the real point of contact for God's Word is the *rectitudo* which through Christ is raised up from real death and thus restored or created anew, and which is real as man's possibility for the Word of God. . . . In faith man is created by the Word of God for the Word of God, existing in the Word of God and not in himself, not in virtue of his humanity and personality.[61]

This passage illuminates an important aspect of the nature of the mutual indwelling. Jesus Christ creates human beings by raising them from the dead and giving them faith by which they actively exist in him. Faith is living outside of oneself in Christ. If Barth has a spirituality, it is this: "Faith never in any respect lives from or by anything other than the Word."[62] In faith, human beings are united to the Word, elevated outside of their own range of possibilities and potential, and given a share in an event which, while real and determinative for their whole existence, does not involve an inward transformation of their humanity as such. Somewhat counter-intuitively, Barth thinks that union with Christ is simultaneously personal and extrinsic—extrinsic, that is, to the human being as *homo peccator*. "The statement about the indwelling of Christ that takes place in faith must not be turned into an anthropological statement. There must be no subtraction from the lostness of natural and sinful man, as whom the believer will for the first time really see himself."[63]

The extrinsic nature of the union accounts for what would otherwise be a tricky problem. As we saw above, Barth adheres to Luther's *simul iustus et peccator* doctrine. But then how can he speak of a real resurrection of *homo peccator* from the dead? If, as Barth asserts, faith does not create a person who is "new in himself, changed in the immanent constitution of his humanity . . . in a depth of his being,"[64] if the regenerate person remains *totus peccator*, then how can the conformity or correspondence to God which takes place in the mutual indwelling be real? Would it not stand to reason that if this union does occur, then it would involve the very sort of inward transformation that Barth denies?

The answer lies in the nature of the union. A human being is as she acts. In herself, apart from union with Christ, she is and acts as a sinner. In Christ, outside of the entire range of possibilities open to her as a sinner, she acts in free faith and obedience as the new creature that the Word has created her to be. She is raised from the dead as she lives in faith, knowl-edge, and obedience—as she exists in union with Christ. Yet her old self always threatens to overtake her new existence in Christ. As the new per-son she is, she remains the old person she was "as an unbeliever *and may become again*."[65] Barth can affirm both real conformity to God and the *totus peccator* because the new human being "exists wholly and utterly by [the Word]. In believing he can think of himself as grounded, not in self but only in this object, as existing indeed only by this object."[66] In the Word, the believer is a new creation. In herself, she remains *totus peccator*. The extrin-sic nature of the union accounts for this.

Mysticism, Not Deification

Interestingly, Barth is not opposed to describing this union, this dying and rising with Christ, as mystical. By *CD* IV he will have changed his mind on this point, claiming that the term "mystical" is too misleading to be a helpful description of the union.[67] But his position here is clear: "The passivity and even death of man in face of the divine act, undoubtedly mean that a mystical vocabulary has already appeared. We should not object to it, for this vocabulary can hardly be avoided at this point."[68] Barth argues that Augustine, Anselm, Bernard of Clairvaux, Luther, and Calvin all affirmed the *"apprehensio Christi* or *habitatio Christi in nobis* or *unio hominis cum Christo* that takes place in real faith according to the teaching of Gal 2:20."[69] "Without this principle," Barth claims, "it is impossible to understand the Reformation doctrine of justification and faith."[70] In the light of Barth's affirmation of the mutual indwelling, it is clear that he carries on this tradition of thought. He carries it on, however, by actualizing it. Barth is careful to distinguish his position from deification: "We do not say a deification [*Vergottung*] but a conformity to God, i.e., an adapting [*Angepaßtsein*] of man to the Word of God."[71] Yet on this point too Barth understood himself to be in agreement with the previous thinkers mentioned. After listing a few quotations from Luther and Augustine which affirm that in *justificatio* a *deificatio* takes place, Barth immediately states that "neither in Augustine nor in Luther is there anything about a deification in faith in the sense of a changing of man's nature into the divine nature."[72] According to Barth, "What makes these expressions possible" for Luther and Augustine is the *"unio hominis cum Christo* that takes place in real faith according to the teaching of Gal 2:20."[73] Barth places them on the side of Calvin in his controversy with Osiander, and he states that Luther and Augustine too would have rejected the Osiandrian "idea of an essential deification of man."[74]

Barth does not go into detail concerning why, in his estimation, these thinkers rejected the idea of an "essential deification." Perhaps that is because to do so would have required him to distinguish his actualistic conception of "essence" from their more traditional conceptions, which would have taken him too far afield. For on a careful reading of the passages in which Barth rejects deification, it turns out that time and again he is arguing against the confusion of divine and human *actions* in the event of union. "If secret identity [*heimliche Identität*] existed here, one would not have to speak of similarity in dissimilarity but of equality in inequality, but then we would not be dealing with mere conformity to God but with a deification of man."[75] Barth is not merely rejecting an unwarranted mixing of divine and human essences considered abstractly. He is rejecting a confusion of divine and human *decisions*—the divine decision of election and the corresponding decision of faith and obedience—and *therefore* divine and human essences. This emphasis accounts for Barth's assessment of the *finitum non capax infiniti* dictum. "As a philosophical saying," Barth declares, "it does not interest us in the slightest."[76] And it does not interest him because he is determined to learn about the nature of the union strictly from the event itself, not from a supposed universally valid metaphysical axiom. Barth affirms the basic insight of the dictum, to be sure, but he does so because of the absolute priority of divine grace: the divine and human decisions are not "equal," because they are determinations that coexist, as we saw earlier, on entirely different levels.[77] Rather than rejecting the saying, he particularizes it according to the event itself: "We do not say *finitum* but *homo peccator non capax*, and we do not continue *infiniti* but *verbi Domini*."[78]

Thus, rather than simply rejecting deification, Barth offers an alternate actualistic conception of the divine-human communion which the doctrine of deification is an attempt to describe. According to Barth, the union between Christ and believers, their mutual indwelling, happens as an event of divine lordship and corresponding human obedience. That is the decisive point revealed in paragraphs five and six.

2

ELECTION AND BEING IN CHRIST

> The doctrine of election is the sum of the Gospel because of all words that can be said or heard it is the best: that God elects man; that God is for man too the One who loves in freedom. It is grounded in the knowledge of Jesus Christ because He is both the electing God and elected man in One. It is part of the doctrine of God because originally God's election of man is a predestination not merely of man but of Himself. Its function is to bear basic testimony to eternal, free and unchanging grace as the beginning of all the ways and works of God.[1]

Barth knew that his Christocentric treatment of election as an aspect of the doctrine of God was unparalleled in the history of Christian theology: "The work has this peculiarity, that in it I have had to leave the framework of theological tradition to a far greater extent than in the first part of the doctrine of God. . . . I was driven irresistibly to reconstruction."[2] In the foreword to *CD* II/2, Barth admits that this work gave him both pleasure (*Freude*) and even greater anxiety (*Sorge*).[3] Given its quality, Barth can hardly be faulted for taking pleasure in it, and his anxiety concerning how the book would be received is perhaps understandable. However, Barth's anxiety clearly does not extend beyond the foreword, and it certainly does not proceed from an ambivalence regarding the legitimacy or successfulness of his treatment of these materials. Yet his satisfaction with his presentation is as nothing compared to his palpable pleasure in the subject matter itself. For while the incisiveness, creativity, scope, and power of his historical, exegetical, ethical, and dogmatic insights will be apparent immediately to anyone who reads the work, his sheer astonishment by and delight in the greatness of the material that he is expounding is perhaps even more striking. Barth makes no attempt to hide his pleasure in the goodness of the things he is describing by concealing it within the rhetorical conventions of detached academic prose. His perception of the reality of God's gracious election in Jesus Christ provided him both knowledge and joy, and he aimed to illuminate this great truth by witnessing to its luminosity. Barth wants the reader to perceive that election is light, not darkness, because Jesus Christ is its content. As both *vere Deus* and *vere homo*, Jesus Christ reveals that to think rightly of election, God, and humanity means to think of them exclusively in light of him and the covenant played out in him. A doctrine of election that fails to adhere to this approach will invariably find itself mired in abysses and labyrinths. But if Jesus Christ is allowed to be the sole criterion of the church's thinking about election, the result is exactly the opposite. Joy, not terror; incomprehensible light, not incomprehensible darkness; clarity, not obscurity, result from the realization that in Jesus Christ God is freely and graciously *for* humanity rather than against it—and, indeed, that this is not merely one variation of God's will, but God's only will for humanity. "The will of God is Jesus Christ . . . we cannot seek any other will of God, either in heaven or earth, either in time or eternity."[4]

In the first part of this chapter, I will treat paragraph thirty-two, which is comprised of three sections. The first, "The Orientation of the Doctrine,"[5] functions as a mini summary of the whole doctrine and sounds the distinctive notes that characterize Barth's approach to the subject. I will give primary attention to this section, with material from the other two sections serving as supporting evidence for my interpretation of this section. In the second part of this chapter, I will discuss paragraph thirty-three, "The Election of Jesus Christ,"[6] which constitutes the heart of Barth's treatment of the doctrine. I will conclude with a brief examination of aspects of the ethical materials in paragraphs thirty-six through thirty-nine which contribute significantly to Barth's overall teaching concerning participation in Christ.

"THE PROBLEM OF A CORRECT DOCTRINE OF THE ELECTION OF GRACE" (*CD* § 32)

Election and the Being of God

The most basic and far-reaching dogmatic point that Barth makes in paragraph thirty-two, and indeed in all of *CD* II/2, is that election is an aspect of the doctrine of God. Election "is part of the doctrine of God because originally God's election of man is a predestination not merely of man but of Himself."[7] Barth's revolution in the doctrine of election is at bottom a revolution in the doctrine of God.[8] Election is an eternal decision, a "primal decision" (*Urentscheidung*) by which God constitutes his being as Lord of the covenant of grace.[9] God is free. Nothing *ad intra* or *ad extra* compelled him to create or redeem the world. But his free and gracious determination to enter into covenant relationship with a reality *ad extra* means that "God is God in this way and not in any other."[10] This decision establishes a relation "which is irrevocable, so that once God has willed to enter into it, and has in fact entered into it, He could not be God without it. It is a relation in which God is self-determined, so that the determination belongs no less to Him than all that He is in and for Himself."[11] In election, God freely constitutes his *being* as the Lord of the covenant.[12]

Even more specifically, Jesus Christ makes this decision. He is both the God who elects and the human being who is elected. Election is a decision made by him as well as one that first of all concerns him. It is gospel for the world, to be sure, but only because humanity is elect in him. But how is this "in him" to be understood?

The answer to this question is located in Barth's teaching concerning the covenant of grace. Jesus Christ's life history is the fulfillment in time of the gracious decision of election in eternity. Election is the ground of Jesus Christ's life history, which is its result. In election:

> what happened was this, that under this name God Himself realized in time, and therefore as an object of human perception, the self-giving of Himself as the Covenant-partner of the people determined by Him from and to all eternity . . . fulfilling [*vollstreckend*] His will upon earth as in the eternal decree which precedes everything temporal it is already fulfilled in heaven.[13]

Thus, according to Barth, Jesus Christ's life history is the covenant of grace, and therefore to be "in him" is to be "in the covenant." "Everything which comes from God takes place 'in Jesus Christ,' i.e., in the establishment of the covenant which, in the union of His Son with Jesus of Nazareth, God has instituted and maintains and directs between Himself and His people. . . ."[14] But how is humanity included in the history of the covenant of grace, and what does that even mean?

Participation in Christ: Its Twofold Form

In a somewhat general sense, Barth's message is unmistakable. Since Jesus Christ is the origin of all things, nothing exists apart from him. He is not accidentally related to all creaturely things, but is their most fundamental presupposition. Jesus Christ encloses (*beschlossen*) the existence and history of humanity within himself. In this sense, everything is "in Jesus Christ." This leads Barth to the radical conclusion that human nature as such does not exist apart from its being in Jesus Christ, apart from its being within the covenant of grace. This claim is analogous to Barth's previous assertion that God is God exclusively within the covenant. While Barth does not make this connection explicit, a similar thought is operative in both cases. Just as election means that "God is God in this way and not in any other,"[15] so too does it mean that there is no such thing as human *being* apart from its being "in Jesus Christ." "There is no such thing as a created nature which has its purpose, being and continuance except through grace."[16] Human nature has no "independent signification."[17]

Yet Barth is clear that this objective (de jure) form of participation in Christ is not the only form. There is also a subjective (de facto) form of participation in Christ. The objective is the more basic of the two forms. It is the ground of the subjective form, which is its consequence and goal—its telos. Moreover, and this is crucial to notice, the nature of objective participation in Christ *guarantees* that participation in Christ will also include a subjective form. Let me explain what these statements mean.

Jesus Christ is the object of election. Humanity benefits from his election by virtue of its being in him. And the meaning of being "in Christ" in the objective sense is that humanity has Jesus Christ as its representative. Consider the following quotations:

1. "If we listen to what Scripture says concerning man, then at the point where our attention and thoughts are allowed to rest there is revealed an elect man, *the* elect man, and united [*vereinigt*] in Him and represented [*vertreten*] by Him an elect people."[18]

2. Jesus Christ is "very man, and as such He is the Representative [*Vertreter*] of the people which in Him and through Him is united as He is with God, being with Him the object of the divine movement."[19]

3. "Jesus Christ is indeed God in His movement towards man, or more exactly, in His movement towards the people represented in the one man Jesus of Nazareth, in His covenant with this people, in His being and activity amongst and towards this people."[20]

Jesus Christ's life, death, and resurrection, his fulfillment of the covenant between God and humanity, are accomplished on behalf of humanity. By being who he is *for* humanity, Jesus Christ establishes, in an objective sense, the being and identity *of* humanity. He establishes, constitutes, and defines human being.

And yet this objectivity is of a very specific sort. De jure participation in Christ does not exclude or replace the action of individual human beings.[21] Rather, it establishes a trajectory for humanity, defining humanity by giving it a telos.[22] In this way, the objective reality of the being of humanity in Christ includes within itself, establishes, and guarantees genuine human subjectivity. In human obedience, the objective aspect of election—the objective presence of the being of humanity in Jesus Christ—is realized in the action of individual human beings "as the *fulfillment* [*Vollzug*] of that prior divine decision."[23] Election and obedience are related to one another as ground and consequence. Jesus Christ's fulfillment of the covenant of grace is a work of faithful obedience. As such it establishes true humanity as a life of faithful obedience. The telos of election is Jesus Christ's life history, and the telos of objective participation in Christ is subjective participation in Christ. In both cases, the telos is realized in obedience.

Participation in God: Sharing as Obedience

According to Barth, in election God wills "to share His life with another" (*mit einem Anderen zusammen sein*).[24] "In entering into this covenant, He freely makes Himself both benefactor [*Wohltäter*] and benefit" (*Wohltat*).[25] Since God shares his life with humanity, human beings receive and participate in God's life, and if they participate in his life, then they participate in his being. How could it be otherwise? But what does it mean to say that human beings share in the being of God?

Barth's answer is straightforward, even if counterintuitive: God gives himself to humanity by making himself the Lord of humanity. "In showing His grace, God proves Himself both Savior and Helper. He does so freely as the Lord. But this exercising of lordship is kind as well as good, communicating and sharing its goods."[26] Grace "rules by offering God to His covenant partner as Lord of the covenant."[27] Here we have a definite explication of the meaning of the statement that God is the benefactor who makes himself the benefit. God offers himself as benefit to the creature— shares his life with the creature—by making himself the Lord of the creature. This relationship of fellowship is very specifically ordered. There is divine action, and there is the human action that it draws forth, and the two are not merged into one another. As obedient human servants of their Lord, human beings participate in the divine life and receive God's self-giving.

> Confronted with the mystery of God, the creature must be silent; not merely for the sake of being silent, but for the sake of hearing. Only to the extent that it attains to silence, can it attain to hearing. But, again, it must be silent not merely for the sake of hearing, but for that of obeying. For obedience is the purpose and goal of hearing. Our return to obedience is indeed the aim of free grace. It is for this that it makes us free. It is for this that it confronts us as a mystery.[28]

In two striking sentences, Barth states that "the mystery [*Geheimnis*] of this election means for the creature that it is set at rest [*Ruhe*]. The rest of decision and obedience; for it is the mystery of the living and life-giving God."[29] Jesus Christ's fulfillment of the covenant of grace eliminates any basis for human anxiety and despair, and it reveals that humanity has been "set at rest." But paradoxically the rest that it has been given is realized actively in obedience.[30]

Yet when Barth says that God shares his life with human beings, does he mean that God gives them something ontologically more than this gift of freedom for active obedience? In other words, does this sharing involve the transformation or healing of human "nature," conceived as a substance that underlies human actions? Or are these actions themselves the creaturely form that God's gift of himself takes? Barth gives every reason to affirm the latter.[31]

By grounding the nature of human sharing in the divine life within the history of the covenant of grace, Barth highlights and insists on the fact that God always remains the Lord of this fellowship. God shares his life with human beings in a way that is appropriate for them as creatures who are not, and never will become, the Lord of the covenant. Since Jesus Christ has secured this fellowship by fulfilling the covenant of grace, fellowship with God can never be abstracted or disconnected from him. He can never be left behind. He is neither the starting point for nor the entrance into some supposedly higher or deeper form of union with God. Nor does the character of this fellowship evolve into some other form of relationship than that between Lord and servants. For Barth, union with God means union with Christ.[32] By elaborating the idea of union with God within the context of the covenant, Barth is attempting to guarantee that the meaning and content assigned to this fellowship will be determined by the meaning and content of Scripture, not secretly nourished by and grounded in some other source.

"THE ELECTION OF JESUS CHRIST" (*CD* § 33)

> In the beginning, before time and space as we know them, before creation, before there was any reality distinct from God which could be the object of the love of God or the setting for His acts of freedom, God anticipated and determined within Himself . . . that the goal and meaning of all His dealings with the as yet non-existent universe should be the fact that in His Son He would be gracious towards man, uniting Himself with him.[33]

Jesus Christ the Savior

Since election is the basis of creation, and creation unfolds from this decision, the meaning and being of the world is defined with respect to this relationship. And yet the people whom God has elected for fellowship with himself have rejected him, and in so doing have forfeited their true being. Their lives have become lies. They are not the people God declares and determines them to be in election. Therefore to exist in this fellowship, to be who they truly are, they need to be rescued. The gospel declares that Jesus Christ has done this. But what qualifies him to be our savior? And how has he done it?

> For where can Jesus Christ derive the authority and power to be Lord and Head of all others, and how can these others be elected "in Him" and how can they see their election in Him the first of the elect, and how can

they find in His election the assurance of their own, if He is only the object of election and not Himself its Subject, if He is only an elect creature and not primarily and supremely the electing Creator? Obviously in a strict and serious sense we can never say of any creature that other creatures are elect "in it," that it is their Lord and Head, and that in its election they can and should have assurance of their own. How can a mere creature ever come to the point of standing in this way before God, above and on behalf of others?[34]

According to Barth, Jesus Christ is fit to be the savior of humanity because he is the subject of election as *vere Deus*. To be sure, were Jesus Christ not *vere homo* he could not be the savior of humanity. But his humanity is of universal significance because he is truly God. Jesus Christ's divinity—not his humanity—is the basis of the universal efficacy and meaning of his humanity.

> From the very beginning (from eternity itself), there are no other elect together with or apart from Him, but, as Eph 1:4 tells us, only "in" Him. "In Him" does not simply mean with Him, together with Him, in His company. Nor does it mean only through Him, by means of that which He as elected man can be and do for them. "In Him" means in His person, in His will, in His own divine choice, in the basic decision of God which He fulfils over against every man. What singles Him out from the rest of the elect, and yet also, and for the first time, unites Him with them, is the fact that as elected man He is also the electing God, electing them in His own humanity. In that He (as God) wills Himself (as man), He also wills them. And so they are elect "in Him," in and with His own election. . . . His election is the original and all-inclusive election [*das ursprüngliche und das komprehensive Erwähltsein*]; the election which is absolutely unique, but which in this very uniqueness is universally meaningful and efficacious [*universal bedeutsame und wirksame*], because it is the election of Him who elects Himself.[35]

Jesus Christ does not represent the whole of humanity—his existence is not of decisive significance for the rest of humanity—because he assumes human "nature" as such and does something in or to it. On this view, objective participation in Christ would mean that human beings share the same essence or substance that the Son of God assumed into his person and healed or cleansed. Such an idea is utterly foreign to Barth's way of thinking. According to Barth, human nature—the *humanum* of every human creature—is something that Jesus Christ *creates* through his life of faith and obedience in fulfillment of the covenant of grace determined from all eternity. What human nature or essence *is* is decided by God in election and is actualized by Jesus Christ in the series of decisions and actions that correspond to that eternal decision and which constitute the history of the covenant. Human nature is as Jesus Christ does it, not as he does something to "it."[36] Thus, Jesus Christ's humanity is "universally meaningful and efficacious" because "He (as God) wills Himself (as man)."[37] If Jesus Christ is not the subject of election, he is not truly God, and if he is not truly God, then he is not qualified to represent humanity, which is elect in him.

With this point in mind, Barth's criticism of traditional views of double-predestination takes on a new significance. Barth's basic argument against, for example, John Calvin and Thomas Aquinas is that they misconstrue "the question of the relationship between predestination and Christology."[38] For Calvin and Thomas, eternal predestination "was set up as a first and independent entity standing over against the center and *telos* of the divine work and of time: a different encounter between God and man than that which became temporal event in Jesus Christ."[39] Barth is convinced that this construal undermines the deity of Jesus Christ.

> Is Jesus Christ really the One who was, and is, and is to come, or is He not? And if He is, what constraint or authority is there that we should not think through to the ultimate meaning of the "He was," not go back to the real beginning of all things in God, i.e., not think of the divine fore-ordination, the divine election of grace, as something which takes place in Him and through Him?[40]

Barth brings the epistemological point to the fore most often throughout his discussion: "If Jesus Christ is only elected, and not only and primarily Elector, what shall we really know at all of a divine electing and our election?"[41] Yet he also thinks that the traditional construal of election cannot support Jesus Christ's work of atonement. Jesus Christ can only reconcile humanity to God if he *is* God, and in order to be God, he must be the subject of election.

But thus far only half of the original question has been answered. I have yet to address *how*, according to Barth, Jesus Christ accomplished our salvation. How, in other words, does atonement work? According to Barth:

> In this one man Jesus, God puts at the head and in the place of all other men the One who has the same power as Himself to reject Satan and to maintain and not surrender the goodness of man's divine creation and destiny. . . . The rejection which all men incurred, the wrath of God under which all men lie, the death which all men must die, God in His love for men transfers from all eternity to Him in whom He loves and elects them, and whom He elects at their head and in their place. God from all eternity ordains this Obedient one in order that He might bear the suffering which the disobedient have deserved and which for the sake of God's righteousness must necessarily be borne. . . . For this reason, He is the Lamb slain, and the Lamb slain from the foundation of the world.[42]

This quote and many others like it reveal that objective participation in Christ is a substitutionary reality. Barth does not think of participation and substitution as alternative ways of conceiving of Christ's atoning work. The two are of a piece with one another. According to Barth:

> In the death which the Son of God has died for them, they themselves have died as sinners. And that means their radical sanctification, separation, and purification for participation in a truly creaturely independence, and more than that, for the divine sonship of the creature which is the grace for which from all eternity they are elected in the election of the man Jesus.[43]

Jesus Christ saves humanity by living, dying, and being raised from the dead *for them* and in their place, and in just that way, sinful humanity is put to death and raised to new life *in him*. Barth brings participation and substitution together in such a way that neither can be described apart from the other: substitution is participatory and participation is substitutionary.

"THE COMMAND OF GOD" (*CD* § 36–39)

Barth makes the transition from dogmatics to ethics in paragraph thirty-six. Yet Barth is obviously not *beginning* to do ethics here. He has already said a great deal about what active participation in covenant fellowship with God means and requires from the human side. He does not simply offer a purely dogmatic section and then follow it with an ethical one. The dogmatic section is full of ethical material, and the ethics is at every point dogmatic. While it is true that "the dogmatics of the Christian Church, and basically the Christian doctrine of God, is ethics,"[44] it is also true that "the propositions of Christian ethics are propositions of Christian dogmatics."[45] Since Christian ethics is undertaken within the context of the covenant that Barth has been describing in the previous paragraphs, paragraph thirty-six does not mark Barth's entrance into fundamentally new territory. The ethical paragraphs are an elucidation and augmentation of the preceding material. "We cannot understand the ethical question," Barth writes, "as the question of human existence as if it were posed in a vacuum, as if there were an ethical question in itself and for itself, as if it were not posed by the grace of God—and not only posed but already answered by the grace of God."[46] When, well into paragraph thirty-seven, Barth sums up a great deal of his teaching concerning the Christological basis of the divine command, we encounter a familiar pattern of thought.

> It is in Jesus that man has this future, and therefore this present task. . . . For it is in Jesus that there has been concluded between God and man the

covenant which forms the beginning of all the ways and works of God, and therefore the objective law under which the existence of all living creatures runs its course. But what will be the relationship to Jesus into which he enters as one upon whom and for whom all this is necessarily valid and binding objectively? Will that which is objectively valid for him become true or not in this relationship? Will it be realized as obedience or as disobedience?[47]

Since so much of the relevant content of the ethical paragraphs has already been treated in the first two sections of this chapter, my treatment of these paragraphs will be different from my approach everywhere else in this study. Rather than examining these paragraphs in detail, I will instead highlight three points which significantly add to what has already been covered. Therefore, the aim of the short section that follows is not to discuss the method and content of Barth's ethics as such, nor is it to attempt to offer anything like a comprehensive assessment of the teaching contained here, but rather to draw out three important contributions which these paragraphs make to Barth's teaching concerning participation in Christ.[48]

The Bond of Union with Christ

The first point concerns the relationship between the divine command and de jure participation in Christ. According to Barth:

The concrete form of this teleological power of grace is the person of Jesus Christ Himself. . . . [A]s He is obedient to this will of God, Jesus also shows what it is that God rightly wills of us. The basic divine decision concerning man is embodied in Jesus. The determination in which man is directed to his promised future, and set in motion towards this future, is given in Him. Jesus Himself is the impulsion of all men to eternal life. He Himself is the claim which God has made and continually makes upon men.[49]

The command of God, which is identical to the person of Christ, is the concrete form in which the teleological power of de jure participation in Christ confronts those for whom Christ is head and representative and in obedience to which they actively participate in him. According to Barth, the command of God is "our bond [Bindung] to the person of Jesus."[50] The command "seeks to bind [binden] us to Jesus Christ in order that in this bond our life may be liberated and free."[51] When this occurs, human obedience becomes the "image and repetition and attestation and acknowledgment" of the covenant of grace, which Jesus Christ fulfilled through his life of total obedience to the will of the Father.[52] Notice how emphatically Barth stresses the totality of Jesus Christ's obedience:

1. As "the Son who is obedient to the Father . . . He is concerned only with obedience."[53]

2. "[I]n what Jesus does everything is genuine obedience, real subordination, even subjection [wirkliche Unterordnung, ja Unterwerfung]—not at all the self-exaltation of man to the throne of God, but very definitely the work of a servant, indeed a slave of God, which takes place in a relationship to God in which God gives the orders and man submits, a position which cannot therefore be reversed."[54]

3. The "obedience of Jesus is the clear reflection of the unity of the Father and the Son by the bond of the Spirit in the being of the eternal God Himself."[55]

Analogously, our union with Christ occurs in obedience to God's command. As Barth writes:

> What we find in the case of the man Jesus is a valid model for the general relationship of man to the will of God. . . . Jesus is obedient to God as the Father in heaven, as the One who wills our salvation and in and with our salvation His glory. And as the Father in heaven, as the One who wills our salvation, God is the Lord of all of us in His Son Jesus Christ, and He wills that we should be obedient to Him.[56]

Moreover, the Son is obedient to the Father by the power of the Holy Spirit, and so too does the Spirit empower human beings to obey God's command.

> As Jesus Christ calls us and is heard by us He gives us His Holy Spirit in order that His own relationship to His Father [i.e., the relationship of obedience] may be repeated [wiederhole] in us [i.e., in our obedience]. He then knows us, and we know Him, as the Father knows Him and He the Father. Those who live in this repetition [Wiederholung] live in the Holy Spirit. The gift and work of the Holy Spirit in us is that Jesus Christ should live in us by faith, that He should be in solidarity and unity with us and we with Him, and therefore that our obedience should be necessary and our disobedience excluded.[57]

It follows from all of this that the command of God is God himself in action drawing human beings into active fellowship. According to Barth, the command of God is a "living command,"[58] a "kind decision" (gütige Entscheidung),[59] because it is the bond of our union with Christ and is the expression of God's love. "The law," Barth famously insists, "is completely enclosed in the gospel."[60]

Abiding in Action

The second point concerns Barth's exegesis of the Johannine passages that speak of believers "abiding" in Christ. Among the many biblical passages that relate to the mutual indwelling between Christ and human beings and upon which an ontology of this mutual indwelling might be based, these passages are especially relevant. But what does it mean to abide in Christ?

Barth observes that "although at a first glance the 'abiding' seems to be merely passive in contrast to a vagabond and vacillating caprice, it, too, impresses the hearer in such a way that there can be no mistaking the fact that it demands obedience and is therefore a command. . . . It is to be realized in their own existence."[61] Barth is not merely saying that God commands us to abide in Christ. He is saying that the mode of this abiding, the manner in which it is "realized," is in *obedience* to the command.[62] To abide in Christ "is something which can take place only through the Yes and No of their own will and determined act."[63] As this occurs "the wholly alien majesty of the new being" vanquishes and supersedes the "old man,"[64] and in this event human beings find that "they are already in the native sphere to which they belong,"[65] since "those who are 'in Christ' already abide in Him, even in the time when they do not actively abide."[66] Barth obviously thinks that these passages can be understood correctly only within the framework of de jure and de facto participation in Christ.

Perfection, Progress, and Perseverance

The final point pertains to the relationship between Christ's reconciling work and our own actions. Since de jure participation in Christ is a teleological reality, the perfection of Jesus Christ's work does not mean that nothing remains for human beings to do. By fulfilling the covenant for us, Jesus Christ does not bring humanity to rest, but sets humanity in motion. Or, using Barth's terminology, Jesus Christ summons humanity to the rest of active obedience. The perfection of Christ's work elicits its fulfillment in our own lives.

Yet Jesus Christ's work really is perfect. He is himself our righteousness, sanctification, and redemption. Thus (and this is important to notice) de facto participation in Christ occurs as the realization of a perfect reality. De facto participation in Christ has the character of an "image and repetition and attestation and acknowledgment"[67] of Jesus Christ's perfect work. This implies that progress is not the best metaphor to describe the Christian life.[68] Since Jesus Christ is himself our righteousness, our righteousness consists in acknowledging his righteousness, in endorsing it as right that he is our righteousness. Likewise, "the divine work of our sanctification for God, the true preparedness for the responsibility which we must fulfill by our action, consists in this—that we should cleave to the salvation accomplished and prepared for us by the death and resurrection of Jesus Christ, and therefore to His sanctity."[69] Or, as Barth puts it elsewhere:

> In relation to the individual what we have to investigate is his participation [Teilnahme] in the righteousness of this Subject, and not his own abstract immanent righteousness. We have to investigate the sanctification that God affects in this Subject, Jesus Christ, not a sanctity of our own which we have to practice and to demonstrate to others. . . . In Him the realization of the good corresponding to divine election has already taken place—and so completely that we, for our part, have actually nothing to add, but have only to endorse [bestätigen] this event by our action.[70]

According to Barth, de jure participation in Christ is both an indicative and an imperative, and the imperative is not episodic, but characterizes every moment of life.[71] The only two possible responses to this imperative are obedience or disobedience. There is no middle term between these two. The command of God confronts humanity in the context of this "inexorable Either-Or" (unerbittliche Entweder-Oder).[72] This leads to Barth's radical claim that "we can live by His grace and compassion, in covenant with Him, *only completely or not at all*."[73] There is nothing partial about this relationship. The idea of a partial righteousness implicit in the idea of progress is out of place in this description. Since "even the obedient are always standing on the edge of the abyss of disobedience, and that this abyss yawns even at their feet,"[74] Barth claims that "the goodness of God—including specifically the goodness of His work for our sanctification—is new every morning. It means that He will again receive and accept us as we are."[75]

Barth's alternative to progress, therefore, is "repetition" or "perseverance." He writes:

> It is to be noted that the continuity of divine grace in our life, and our obedience to it, will be maintained only in so far as we do not refuse the discipline of the new beginning of our life and understanding brought about by moral reflection. The continuity of a life which steadily affirms itself from one decision to another, developing from within itself, can only be the continuity of disobedience. For the law which governs the life of the Church is repeated in every individual life. . . . The principle of necessary repetition and renewal [das Gesetz der notwendigen Wiederholung und Erneuerung], and not a law of stability, is the law of spiritual growth [Wachstums] and continuity [Kontinuität] in our life. It is when we observe this law that we practice perseverance [Beharrlichkeit] (ὑπομονή) in the biblical meaning of the term; a perseverance corresponding to the steadfastness of God Himself.[76]

Christians rely upon God's steadfast faithfulness, not their own inward righteousness. Thus, Barth concludes that as human beings are obedient, "they may and must make progress as those who unfailingly hope."[77]

By rejecting the idea that growth in the Christian life means a gradual increase in one's own inward righteousness, Barth underscores the perfection and sufficiency of Jesus Christ's righteousness for humanity. He does not, however, intend to undermine the urgency of obedience or endorse a laissez-faire attitude concerning the daily—indeed the moment to moment—need to die to oneself and live to God. Neither does he denigrate wisdom and maturity. Barth thinks that the urgency of unceasing obedience can be safeguarded just as well with the concepts of repetition and perseverance as it can with that of progress. Indeed, by emphasizing the proximity of the peril of the abyss of disobedience, Barth wants his readers to appreciate the gravity of every moment of life. At root, his position is an assault on all forms of complacency in the Christian life. It is an attempt to draw attention to the fact that the Christian life is lived in absolute, active, and moment-to-moment dependence upon God.

This point serves as a fitting and emphatic conclusion to the material set forth in this chapter. Barth's description of perseverance is an implication of his covenantal construal of participation in Christ. Having freely and graciously decided in election to be the God of the covenant, Jesus Christ establishes the being of humanity through his representative fulfillment of the covenant on our behalf. Moreover, his being for us, and therefore our being in him, is teleologically ordered toward the faith and obedience by which we become those whom he has graciously established that we are and will be. God binds us to Jesus Christ in the power of the Holy Spirit, such that our lives of obedience, proleptically included in his life for us, become repetitions of his obedience to the Father and thereby realize their telos.

3

HUMAN NATURE IN CHRIST

In the preface to *CD* III/2, Barth writes that his "exposition deviates even more widely from dogmatic tradition than in the doctrine of predestination in II,2. None of the older or more recent fathers known to me was ready to take the way to a theological knowledge of man which I regard as the only possible one."[1] Having seen in the previous chapter something of the innovative genius of Barth's doctrine of election, this statement becomes all the more striking. But what exactly is this singularly necessary and yet previously neglected way to knowledge in the area of theological anthropology?

The answer is given in a sentence expressing the thought that forms the basis of *CD* III/2 as a whole and informs all of its constituent parts: "The ontological determination of humanity is grounded in the fact that one man among all others is the man Jesus."[2] Barth's deviation from tradition is rooted in a single, simple, and spectacularly wide-ranging presupposition—that Jesus Christ alone establishes and reveals human nature. Barth's anthropology is an attempt to take this thought seriously, to follow it wherever it may lead, and to resist the temptation to either deviate from it or stop short of saying what must be said on the basis of it. Knowledge drawn from any other source, no matter how true or helpful, will only describe the "phenomenon" of human nature, never human nature as such. We are faced here with a striking example of Barth's commitment to the dictum *Latet periculum in generalibus!*—"Danger lurks in generalities!"[3]

But Barth's statement that he is deviating even more widely from dogmatic tradition than he did in the doctrine of election can be misleading. If it is correct that Barth's particularism—his insistence on thinking through the subject matter consistently from this starting point—is what necessitates his "deviation" from the dogmatic tradition, then this deviation is not the result of a new development in his thought, but rather is forced upon him by an assumption already securely in place. In the preface to *CD* II/2 Barth makes a comment similar to the one he makes here.

There he notes that he "had to leave the framework of theological tradition to a far greater extent" than was necessary in the first volume and than he would have liked to have done.[4] And yet why did he feel it necessary to make this departure within the doctrine of election? Was it not for the same reason that he felt it necessary to deviate from the dogmatic tradition in the area of theological anthropology?

Barth may or may not have been correct that the contents of *CD* III/2 are more innovative than those in *CD* II/2. Yet the Christocentric orientation so clearly worked out in the doctrine of election is certainly what led him to develop the theological anthropology that he did. The doctrine of election is where the decision was made that there exists no independent relationship between God and creation apart from Jesus Christ. As Barth expresses it in *CD* III/1, the covenant is the "internal basis of creation," whereas creation is the "external basis of the covenant."[5] Since no general—i.e., non-Christological—relation exists between God and creation, there can be no general—i.e., non-Christological—anthropology. As Barth filled out the anthropology that was already present (both implicitly and explicitly) in *CD* II/2, he took up new themes and developed the material in important ways, but he always did so in accordance with the trajectory he set for himself in the doctrine of election. Thus, whereas it was necessary in the previous chapter to offer a broad and somewhat detailed description of the material most relevant to the topic of participation in Christ by drawing from numerous paragraphs within *CD* II/2, that is not the case in this chapter. Many of the key ideas informing Barth's anthropology in *CD* III/2 were set forth in the previous chapter on election, and thus need not be repeated here. Rather than drawing widely from across *CD* III/2, this chapter will offer a focused reading of the very rich and important section titled "The Real Man" (*Der wirkliche Mensch*).[6]

This chapter makes four major contributions to the study as a whole. First, it demonstrates the deep continuity between Barth's understanding of participation in Christ in the second and third volumes of *Church Dogmatics*. Second, and most broadly, it defines exactly what Barth means by "history," and it shows why that category is so important for him. Third, and closely related, it establishes that Barth is not working with a *traditional* two natures Christology (a point that I will explore in greater detail in chapter 5), but with a thoroughly actualized conception of both the "natures" and the "person" of the union, in which the latter is the dynamic history of the one Son of God and the man Jesus. Finally, this chapter clarifies the reason for Barth's rejection of substantialist understandings of human nature, and it shows that the active and historical character of subjective participation in Christ is grounded in Barth's specific understanding of the hypostatic union.

"THE REAL MAN" (*CD* § 44.3)

The Irreducible Fact of Human Nature

Barth begins by offering his central thesis: "The ontological determination [*ontologische Bestimmung*] of humanity is grounded in the fact that one man among all others is the man Jesus."[7] Or, as he puts it a few pages later, it is "ontologically decisive [*ontologisch entscheidend*] that one man among all others is the man Jesus."[8] In order to know what human nature is, one must look to the place where it has been once and for all enacted and definitively established. Jesus Christ is "the one Archimedian point given us beyond humanity, and therefore the one possibility of discovering the ontological determination of man."[9] In the election of Jesus Christ and its fulfillment in time, "a decision has been made concerning the being and nature [*Sein und Wesen*] of every man by the mere fact that" Jesus Christ himself is a human being.[10]

This thought is so simple as almost to be elusive. The irreducible fact of human nature is that Jesus Christ is a human being (not some other supposedly defining human characteristic such as rationality, responsibility, existence in relationship, or anything else). Jesus Christ's fulfillment of the covenant of grace establishes the context within which human beings exist, and that context is determined fundamentally by the relationship of lordship and obedience that Jesus Christ embodies. Thus election, covenant, Christology, anthropology, history, participation, and ontology are all inextricably linked. The essence of human life is to be drawn into the covenant, to exist within the sphere of this relationship. Jesus Christ is himself the relationship of the transcendent Lord and the perfectly obedient servant. The occurrence of this relationship constitutes his history. Therefore, human life is life "in him," life in the history of this relationship.[11]

Human Nature as Summons

Barth develops this thesis by claiming that to be human is to be summoned by the Word of God.

> Among all other men and all other creatures He is the penetrating spearhead of the will of God their Creator: penetrating because in Him the will of God is already fulfilled and revealed, and the purpose of God for all men and creatures has thus reached its goal; and the spearhead to the extent that there has still to be a wider fulfillment of the will of God and its final consummation, and obviously this can only follow on what has already been achieved in this man.[12]

The teleological character of objective participation in Christ which emerged in the last chapter is present again here. In Jesus Christ, the will of God is already fulfilled and revealed as the purpose for all humanity—indeed humanity is "penetrated" by it. But this objective reality takes the form of a "spearhead," an impetus for the rest of humanity "to be a wider fulfillment of the will of God." This fulfillment happens as human beings respond to Jesus Christ's call to discipleship. This leads Barth to conclude that human beings do not

> have a kind of nature in which they are then addressed by God. They do not have something different and earlier and more intrinsic [*Eigentliches*], a deeper stratum or more original substance of being [*keine tiefere Schicht, keine ursprüngliche Substanz seines Seins*], in which they are without or prior to the Word of God. They are from the very outset, as we may now say, "in the Word of God." They are beings which are summoned [*aufgerufenes*] by the Word of God and to that extent historical, grounded in the history inaugurated in this Word. And whatever else their nature may be, it is subordinated to this historicity and explicable only in the light of it.[13]

When the reality of human nature is in question, the word "real" is simply equivalent to "summoned."[14]

Barth warns that it may seem appropriate to inquire into the identity of the being who is thus summoned: Who is the being that God claims in this way? Who was this being prior to being summoned? Yet such questions arise only if one misunderstands or denies the initial premise. Barth's point is that human nature has no existence prior to this summons. To raise such questions, whether wittingly or unwittingly, is an attempt "to explain ourselves by ourselves instead of by our concrete confrontation with God,"[15] and "perhaps the fundamental mistake in all erroneous thinking of man about himself is that he tries to equate himself with God and therefore to proceed on the assumption that he can regard himself as the presupposition of his own being."[16] In strict opposition to such thinking, Barth argues that a human being "is a man as he is summoned, and his endowment merely follows as part of the summons, his constitution being his equipment."[17]

Being and History

In what turns out to be the first and most complex point in a series of recapitulations in which Barth builds on what he calls the "two material and therefore primary statements"[18] of the discussion—namely, that humanity derives from God's election and has its being in the hearing of the Word of God—he claims that "the being of man is a history."[19] Barth defines history by contrasting it with what he calls a state (*Zustand*). According to Barth, the concept of a state "involves the idea of something completely insulated within the state in question, the idea of a limitation of its possibilities and therefore of its possible changes and modes of behavior."[20] Thus, a being within a state includes some intrinsic element that is self-consistent and perdures unchanged beneath all change, and this being is limited to the movements that are intrinsic to the state itself. On the other hand, whereas a being in a state remains forever insulated within its own limits, history occurs as these limits are transcended by an outside factor.

> History, therefore, does not occur when the being is involved in changes or different modes of behavior intrinsic to itself, but when something takes place upon and to the being as it is. The history of a being begins, continues and is completed when something other than itself and transcending its own nature encounters it, approaches it and determines its being in the nature proper to it, so that it is compelled and enabled to transcend itself in response and in relation to this new factor. The history of a being occurs when it is caught up in this movement, change and relation, when its circular movement is broken from without by a movement towards it and the corresponding movement from it, when it is transcended from without so that it must and can transcend itself outwards [wenn es von außen überschritten wird, um dann auch sich selber nach außen überschreiten zu müssen und zu können].[21]

Thus, history occurs as a being in a state is encountered by a different kind of being and when the being thus encountered responds correspondingly with an action that is not within the range of its own inherent possibilities. The difference between a history and a state is not that the latter is not dynamic or involves no change, but rather that the movement that takes place within a state is generated from within that state, is intrinsic to that state, whereas for an event to be "historical" it requires a transcendent action that intersects and interrupts the state. Furthermore, if this is the case, if a being in a state has such a history, then the nature of that being is located within the history itself. It has no nature in and for itself, because its existence is not isolated, but rather occurs in relationship with the transcending factor. A being with a history is as this history occurs, and its nature is therefore located wholly within the history. In fact, according to Barth, "it is quite inappropriate to say that this being has a history (as though it merely happened to have this history in addition to what it is)."[22]

After offering these rather technical definitions, Barth proceeds to show that they derive directly from the existence of Jesus Christ. Indeed, apart from him, all extant beings could be fully described within the concept of a state—as beings variously described according to the inherent limits of their own possibilities. In Jesus Christ, however, we are "forced" to apply the concept of history. In a passage that is as rich in its implications as any

other in this part-volume, if not in the entire *Church Dogmatics*, Barth
describes Jesus Christ as follows:

> At this point being is not simply movement within itself. It is not confined
> to the sphere of the specific possibilities characteristic of a specific being.
> It is both the transcendence and transcending of such a sphere—its tran-
> scendence by a new and different factor and its transcending in response
> and relation to this factor. It is the identity of the Creator and creature. And
> the Creator is for the creature the utterly new and other. If it is the case
> that the man Jesus is Himself the Creator who has become creature, then
> He exists in a manner which cannot be exhaustively described by any
> state, but in Him we are faced by the fulfillment of the strict concept of
> history. For it is really not a state that the Creator and creature are one. In
> consideration of the otherness and newness of the Creator in relation to
> the creature, we can understand it only as history. This creature is what it
> is as creature in a dynamic movement[23] of the Creator to itself and itself
> to the Creator. It exists in this movement from another to itself to this
> other—a movement which, since God the Creator is this Other, it is quite
> impossible to describe as a movement within itself. And since it repre-
> sents itself as a being of this kind, it clearly forbids us to seek its essence
> behind or apart from this movement. It does not "have" a history from
> which it can itself be distinguished as a substratum. But it "is" in this his-
> tory, i.e., it is, as it takes place that the Creator is creature and the creature
> Creator. . . . Its being as such, the being of the man Jesus, lies in the fact
> that God is for Him and He for God. And we remember what all this
> means—that in the existence of this man it takes place that God takes up
> the cause of His threatened creature. There comes upon the creature the
> new fact that above and beyond its actual being God gives Himself to it
> as the Deliverer in order that it may itself be the Deliverer. There comes
> upon it the fact that it is elected by God and may therefore elect Him in
> return. . . . Jesus exists only in this history, i.e., in this history of the
> covenant and salvation and revelation inaugurated by God in and with
> the act of creation. Jesus is, as this history takes place.[24]

This passage is illuminating in many ways. However, for our purposes
only two observations need to be made concerning it.

First, Barth clearly is not operating here with a traditional "two natures"
Christology. Or, perhaps more precisely, Barth's understanding of both the
natures and the person of the union is highly original, if not unprece-
dented. To say that the Son of God assumed a human nature is not to say
that the Son of God assumed a substance that could otherwise be described
apart from this act of assumption. Instead, it means that the Son of God
lives as a man, indeed, the man he was always elected to be. Barth is not
simply affirming the *anhypostatic* and *enhypostatic* character of Jesus
Christ's human nature. Traditionally, that *theologoumenon* was affirmed as
a defense against adoptionism. Barth's point is that there is no humanity

at all apart from the act of this union. Indeed, the hypostatic union is itself the history of the dynamic relationship between God and humanity in one person, a relationship that defines humanity itself.[25] Jesus Christ is in his one person the history of the movement from the Creator to the creature and back again, the history of sovereign lordship and free obedience as it happens. Jesus Christ never contradicts himself with sin, and therefore he is the only one about whom it may be said that he is always truly human. His identity—the person of the union—is always the uninterrupted dynamic movement of divine lordship and human obedience.

The second observation is related to the first. If the union of divine and human natures in Jesus Christ occurs as the actions of this history occur— as the actions of the divine Lord draw forth the freely faithful and obedient actions of the man Jesus—the union of believers with Jesus Christ can be expected to occur in analogy to this dynamic movement. As the summons of the Lord is met with the free obedience of his servants, history occurs and human being is actualized. To be sure, Jesus Christ's history is "primal history,"[26] and the history of those whom he represents "is clearly history in a secondary, derivative and indirect sense of the term."[27] But the hypostatic union is "historical," and so too is human fellowship with God, and thus Barth argues that "it is really not a state that the Creator and the creature are one."[28] Barth describes the event of human fellowship with God in a variety of ways: the transcending of human beings by God and the corresponding human transcendence of one's state; the procession of divine action and the return of fitting human action; the divine election of humanity and the human election of God, and so on. All these ways of speaking point to the same event: the union of God and humanity that occurs as God's command is met with human obedience. Thus, Barth concludes that "the formula that man is 'in the Word of God' does not denote a mere state, but the being of man as history."[29]

Sin as Nonbeing

Barth's final recapitulation of the material is a discussion of the concept of responsibility (*Verantworlichkeit*). Prior to this discussion, he makes a point that will allow us to address an important question. Barth argues that the term responsibility does not "denote a state of being characterized by a particular potentiality, but an act and occurrence and therefore the being itself."[30] The being of humanity is not located in the existence of the mere possibility of responsibility, but in its actualization, in its use. "What makes him real man is that he is engaged in active responsibility to God. He would not be real man if his responsibility were not actualized as history."[31] But what about the person who fails to give this action? Is Barth saying that such a person ceases to be a human being? Furthermore, if he is, then what is the constant in each human life that underlies the unique identity of each human creature irrespective of the character of his actions?

If these questions were posed to Barth, his answers would proceed from the starting point of the distinction between objective and subjective participation in Christ. He would respond that, yes, when one fails to give this action, one ceases to be a human being—i.e., one ceases to act as a human being. When this occurs, the creature contradicts her own humanity and embraces nonbeing. To sin is to cease to act as a human being and therefore to cease to *be* human. Barth's actualism must not be watered down: human being is in-act and not otherwise. However, once this has been said, Barth's objectivism immediately comes to the fore. While the sad fact is that human beings contradict their own humanity, such action does not invalidate, overwhelm, or dissolve the fact that Jesus Christ has claimed and secured the humanity of each and every individual. Perhaps a clear way to put this point is to say that human beings are not always themselves. Or, more precisely, even if somewhat cryptically, human beings are not always who they really are, and therefore they *are* not. The constant which underlies the identity of each human being is the objective participation of humanity in Jesus Christ, which proceeds from election, is secured in the life history of Jesus Christ, and is ever-present in teleological power.[32] Where and when human action corresponds to God's gracious command as it confronts the individual in each moment of her life, she is living as the human being she really is. When a person fails to offer this free obedience, she contradicts her own being and she ceases to be in herself who she really is in Christ.[33] Nevertheless, sin does not create a new and independent reality for human nature apart from its reality in Jesus Christ. Sin is merely the evil and absurd denial of that reality.

The "Inner Notes" of Responsibility

Barth concludes with an examination of what he calls the "inner notes" of responsibility.[34] As the Word of God declares itself and is known, "the history inaugurated by God becomes man's own subjective history."[35] As this happens, human beings participate in the Word. A person "is, as he is responsible before God, and thus has a share [*Anteil*] in the Word of God and therefore in God Himself—a creaturely share in a creaturely manner, but nevertheless a real share. Man is the context (*Zusammenhang*) of this process of knowledge which comes from God and returns to Him."[36] God is known as people are given a share in Jesus Christ's history, as they are awakened to the fact that their true identity is found in him, and as they embrace and enact that identity in grateful response to this fact. When this happens, human beings "move Godwards out of themselves,"[37] and in so doing they see themselves in this process. They "detach themselves from themselves,"[38] and thus they become an object to themselves. Such self-knowledge, Barth argues, accompanies the knowledge of God as its shadow.[39] In fact, it is impossible to truly know oneself outside of this process. "The simple and pregnant statement: 'I am' . . . is not an independent affirmation. It is not absolutely true. We can dare affirm it only to the accompaniment and in consequence of the affirmation: 'God is.'"[40]

Barth does not devote a great deal of attention to this point, nor does he draw out any of its entailments. Yet this line of thought is a development of his extrinsically oriented spirituality of the Word of God. Previously I argued that Barth upholds the particular concern undergirding the development within the Christian tradition of the concept of infused habits without adopting the concept or any of the attendant ontologies within which it was developed.[41] Similarly, in the present context, Barth is acknowledging the valid concern of inwardly directed spiritualities. Barth understands the wisdom of the Socratic dictum: "Know thyself," and he agrees with its translation into Christian spirituality. However, like Calvin before him, he always presses us to see that only as we look away from ourselves toward God will we ever really know ourselves. No matter how important knowledge of self is, it is secondary in importance to knowledge of God. And not only is it secondary in importance, self-knowledge is impossible apart from knowledge of God, because our basic identity is determined by God in election and actualized in our response to election.

Barth next highlights a point that has proven central throughout this study. "As the being of man is being in responsibility before God, it has the character of obedience to God."[42] In this context, Barth emphasizes the *active* character of obedience:

> That he is, and is therefore obedient, means that the statement: "I am," must be interpreted by the further statement: "I will." . . . Man is, of course, purely receptive [*rein rezeptiv*] as regards the movement from God, but he is also purely spontaneous [*rein spontan*] in the movement to God. . . . God is Subject, but over against God and in relation to Him man is also subject. . . . By willing, I recognize the fact that my being is not simply a gift with which I am endowed but a task for which I am commissioned. Indeed, I affirm and grasp my being as my task, and treat it as such.[43]

To will is not merely to agree that a course of action is right, but to engage in that action; not simply to desire, plan, or contemplate a certain decision, but to make the decision. "'I am,' requires further explanation. It means: 'I do.'"[44] To will obedience is to "dare to step out into the new sphere of my future, leaving what I was and moving to what I shall be, on the path which was indicated for me by my origin, and on which I can proceed only as active and acting subject."[45] Thus Barth concludes that "the obedient man—and properly and in truth only he—knows what he is saying when he says: 'I am.'"[46]

In the event of this response, human being has the character of an "invocation (*Anrufung*) of God."[47] Upon making this claim, Barth offers an important clarification regarding the nature of the history in which humanity has its being.

> The grace of God and the gratitude of man, the Word of God and the response of man, the knowledge and act of God and those of man, take place on two very different levels and in two very different ways [*auf zwei ganz verschiedenen Ebenen und je in ihrer eigenen Art*] which even in the content of this history are not the same and are not interchangeable. God transcends the limits of the creature in one way, and man in another.[48]

God's action within this history is sovereign and majestic. Human action is dependent and humble. Human beings transcend the limits of their state not by being elevated to a level higher than that of a creature, but by actively participating in the history of the covenant. Transcending the limits of one's state does not mean to become divine. It means to do something as a creature that the creature cannot do on its own—to decide for God in response to God's decision for the creature. Utterly dependent upon God, human beings are permitted to entrust themselves to God and place themselves at his disposal. They are free to invoke God's mercy, submit to God's judgment, and cling to God's promise of salvation. Thus, while it is difficult to imagine an anthropology with more emphasis on action, in the final analysis human beings are forced to wait on the Lord. It is only in the humility of waiting that human action reaches its goal: "As man invokes God as his Judge and awaits His verdict, the circle is closed."[49]

Barth sums up the discussion with a reflection on responsibility as freedom. "Because it is so comprehensive, the concept of freedom must be the limit beyond which real man can only be seen and no longer defined or described."[50] Barth's statements about freedom are deeply rooted in the Augustinian heritage of the Christian tradition. Freedom exists only in its exercise. It is not a neutral capacity for choice in one direction or another, but is "actualized and exercised only in the knowledge of God, in obedience to him."[51] Barth is making essentially the same claim about freedom that he made previously about responsibility: like responsibility, freedom is only an attribute of human nature as it is actualized in the history that constitutes human nature. And this, of course, brings us back once again to Christology and participation in Christ.

There is no human life, Barth is arguing, apart from active correspondence to Jesus Christ. That is the whole thrust of his actualistic anthropology—his insistence that human nature is a history and not, as he once again reminds the reader under this final heading, "a substance with certain qualities or functions."[52] Barth's basic, and really his only, argument against substantialist—i.e., nonhistorical (in the Barthian sense of the term)—accounts of human nature is that they fail either to perceive or to take seriously the fact that humanity derives exclusively from election, has no independent existence apart from Jesus Christ, and is actualized in faith and obedience.

Thus, this chapter ends where it began, by arguing that Barth's anthropology proceeds from his doctrine of election and is characterized from beginning to end by *geschichtlich* thinking. As we now turn our attention to Barth's doctrine of reconciliation, it will become apparent immediately that the whole volume, and each of its constituent parts, is worked out in the same historical-covenantal way. The deep continuity that marks the presentation of participation in Christ in the second and third volumes of the *Church Dogmatics* likewise holds true for the fourth. In fact, the most conspicuous, innovative, and brilliant feature of Barth's doctrine of reconciliation is his determined attempt to retranslate the whole of it into a history, to allow his thinking to be governed at every point by its dynamic center in Jesus Christ. The result is a magisterial presentation of reconciliation as an event of pure movement. That material will occupy our attention for the final two chapters of this study.

4

THE GRACE OF GOD IN CHRIST

While the Christocentric orientation of Barth's theology is in place from the beginning of the *Church Dogmatics*, he does not offer his full-scale treatment of the person and work of Christ until the fourth volume—the doctrine of reconciliation. And he begins with a sober recognition of the task that lies before him: "To fail here is to fail everywhere," he writes, for the doctrine of reconciliation is nothing less than "the center of all Christian knowledge . . . the heart of the Church's dogmatics."[1] Yet despite his obvious awe before the subject matter, one quickly realizes that Barth has lost none of his characteristic mettle. "There is no theology without risk," he loudly declares, as he proceeds to chart his unique course through this important material.[2]

Rather than dividing the person and work of Christ into discrete chapters, Barth sets out to integrate the two into a unified whole, offering a description of Christ's "active person or his personal work."[3] He reshapes and interweaves the states of humiliation and exaltation, the threefold office, and the ontological constitution of the Mediator into a single fabric.[4] Since the Holy Spirit is "the power in which Jesus Christ attests Himself,"[5] this volume also includes Barth's most extensive pneumatology. Likewise, since the atonement is the history of Jesus Christ in whom the whole of humanity participates, Barth offers lengthy sections on sin, the church, faith, hope, love, justification, sanctification, and vocation, as well as a partially completed ethics of reconciliation. The scope and ambition of this project is staggering. Of course, the degree to which Barth succeeds in all of this is another matter. But the quality of Barth's achievement has led one recent interpreter to go as far as to claim that "Barth's doctrine of reconciliation is one of a handful of post-Reformational theological works with clear title to classic status."[6]

CD IV/1: OVERVIEW

Barth divides *CD* IV/1 into two "chapters." The first, chapter thirteen, is especially useful in that it offers a survey not just of this part-volume, but

of the doctrine of reconciliation as a whole. Like all of Barth's prolegomena, it introduces the doctrine of reconciliation by expounding it. Chapter
fourteen, which forms the bulk of *CD* IV/1, approaches the material from
the perspective of the self-humiliation of God. Its title—"Jesus Christ, the
Lord as Servant"—makes that clear. Here Barth views the one event of reconciliation from the perspective of Jesus Christ as the Son of God who is
vere Deus precisely as he fulfills the covenant of grace by rendering full obedience to the Father and being judged in the place and for the sake of sinners (§59).[7] Sin, therefore, when considered in the light of the obedience of
the Son of God, takes the form of pride: those for whom the Lord became
a servant themselves desire to become the Lord (§60). On the other hand,
and in immediate contrast to this, the faith that justifies acknowledges a
reality independent of one's own faith: the death of sinful humanity as
such in the death of Jesus Christ (and therefore one's own death) and the
establishment of true humanity in his resurrection (and therefore one's
own true life) (§61). Gathered by the Holy Spirit, the church is the community awakened to this truth as it has come to all humanity in Jesus Christ
(§62), a truth which the church actively receives and affirms in faith (§63).
In *CD* IV/1, Barth approaches reconciliation from the perspective of the
deity of Jesus Christ; the priestly office; sin as pride; justification, and faith.[8]

Within *CD* IV/1, three sections are especially relevant to the theme of participation in Christ. The first is paragraph fifty-seven. Titled "God with Us,"[9]
this section contains what Barth refers to as "the core [*Kern*] of the Christian
message,"[10] and is crucial for specifying Barth's ontology of participation in
Christ. The second two sections are both located in paragraph fifty-eight. In
"The Grace of God in Jesus Christ,"[11] Barth severely criticizes Roman
Catholic conceptions of grace, while offering a covenantal-actualistic alternative, which simultaneously affirms that Jesus Christ alone is grace (and
therefore grace is and always remains *aliena*) and that believers are themselves transformed in active participation in Christ. In "The Being of Man in
Jesus Christ,"[12] Barth discusses the three aspects of the one grace of Jesus
Christ (justification, sanctification, and calling), which together constitute
the objective being of humanity in Christ. This section is especially helpful
in that Barth illuminates the interconnections between these topics by treating them all at once.

In addition to these three sections, the transitional discussion "The Verdict of the Father" could also have been treated.[13] In that section, Barth
addresses the *Lessingfrage* with a description of Jesus Christ's resurrection.
De jure participation in Christ, Barth argues, is "a given major" from which
de facto participation in Christ may be deduced as "a minor and conclusion."[14] The former is a perfect work "which needs no amplification," yet
the latter really occurs as Jesus Christ attests himself in the power of his resurrection.[15] According to Barth, Lessing's question "is not simply technical

or logical or methodological."[16] It is not simply the question of the relationship between faith and history. Given what has been accomplished in Jesus Christ—the end of sinful humanity in his death and the establishment of the new future of humanity in his resurrection—the question becomes existential and ontological too: "To be or not to be is the question now."[17] The transition from death to life has already taken place in Jesus Christ, and as "the living Mediator between God and man in the power of His resurrection" he awakens people to this truth, making them alive in the process.[18] He grants them faith in his living presence and hope in his final Parousia, and creates them into a community of witnesses to his death and resurrection. Thus Barth's answer to Lessing's question emerges: having been raised from the dead, Jesus Christ is eternally alive as the Representative and Advocate for all people in all times and places: "There is no moment in which Jesus Christ is not Judge and High Priest. . . . There is no moment in which this perfect tense is not present. . . . The eternal action of Jesus Christ in His resurrection is itself the true and direct bridge from once to always, from Himself in His time to us in our time."[19] While treating this section in more detail would have been helpful, I have decided instead to examine Barth's baptism fragment in the conclusion of this study. In that part-volume, Barth presents an argument concerning the relationship between de jure and de facto participation in Christ that is very similar to the one he offers in "The Verdict of the Father." In addition to presenting that argument, treating the baptism fragment will allow me to offer a brief explanation of why baptism and the Lord's Supper do not appear in this study.

Paragraph Fifty-seven

Anyone who reads CD IV/1 will notice that it contains two introductions—paragraphs fifty-seven and fifty-eight. Moreover, paragraph fifty-eight is a rather detailed "survey" of the doctrine of reconciliation, which easily could have stood alone as an introduction to the entire fourth volume. But Barth chose to preface it with another survey of the doctrine. Why? As far as I know, no one has ever attempted to answer this question.

According to Barth, "Jesus Christ is the atonement."[20] Apart from the fellowship established between God and humanity in him, neither God nor humanity is. Reconciliation, the fulfillment of the covenant between God and humanity, "is an event in Jesus Christ."[21] The aim of paragraph fifty-seven is to sear that fact into the reader's mind. The covenant is "the basis and essence, the ontological substance of the original relationship between God and man."[22] The covenant, according to Barth,

> is the first thing we have to recognize and say about God and man in their relationship one with another. . . . From all eternity God elected and

determined that He Himself would become man for us men. From all eternity He determined that men would be those for whom He is God: His fellow-men. In willing this, in willing Jesus Christ, He wills to be our God and He wills that we should be His people. *Ontologically*, therefore, the covenant of grace is already included and grounded in Jesus Christ, in the human form and human content which God willed to give His Word from all eternity.[23]

In Jesus Christ, "God has elected and determined Himself as the fellow and friend of man, and elected and determined man as His own friend and fellow. . . . Man has his *real being* in the fact that his existence was willed and is actual in this meaning and purpose. . . . He *is* in virtue of the covenant already concluded with God."[24] This covenantal construal of the relationship of divine and human being is at the heart of Barth's ontology of participation in Christ, and paragraph fifty-seven is an extended ontological preface to the entire doctrine of reconciliation. It functions as a set of ontological guidelines, ground rules, and parameters within which Barth intends his teaching concerning divine-human fellowship to be understood. Salvation is a matter of union and communion with God in Christ, and thus it is a matter of being. Therefore, the successfulness of an interpretation of Barth's understanding of this fellowship will largely depend on how accurately one perceives the ontology of this event.

"GOD WITH US" (*CD* § 57.1)

The Possibility of Sharing in God

In this section, Barth offers a series of observations, all of which elaborate the meaning of the confession: "God with us." While Barth does not point this out, the alert reader will notice that the thread that links these observations is a description of divine-human fellowship as a mutual participation of divine and human being—a communion of mutually shared being. Each observation highlights and describes a different aspect of this fellowship.

Barth begins by pointing out that the confession "'God with us' . . . is not a state but an event."[25] God "is who He is, and lives as what He is, in that He does what He does."[26] As such, God's being is "incomparable" (*unvergleichlich*).[27] Yet, if this is so, an important question immediately arises. This assertion seems to imply that God's being is incommunicable. If God's being is in-act, how can God share his being without ceasing to be the God he is or creating another God alongside himself? If the act in which God exists is always sovereign and gracious, how can he share his being with another? Moreover, if Barth's actualistic premises entail the conclusion that the divine being cannot be shared, then the whole presentation founders, since its thesis is that such sharing actually takes place. In other words, Barth's own premises seem to rule out the point he is most concerned to make.

This is a helpful way of framing the issue because according to Barth the divine being *cannot* be shared in the way that this line of questioning assumes. That is, if Barth tells us that God's being is in his sovereign act, and he also tells us that God shares his being with humanity, then we would expect him to mean that God shares his being with humanity in a way that is suitable for creatures who are not, and never will become, God. And that is precisely what Barth argues throughout this section. But how does God share his being with humanity?

According to Barth, he does so by including humanity in the history of the covenant. God with us means "that we ourselves are in the sphere of God."[28]

> The divine being and life and act takes place with ours, and it is only as the divine takes place that ours takes place. To put it in the simplest way, what unites God and us men is that He does not will to be God without us, that He creates us rather to share with us and therefore with our being and life and act His own incomparable being and life and act, that He does not allow His history to be His and ours, but causes them to take place as a common history [*gemeinsame Geschichte*].[29]

As this common history takes place, God shares himself with us. In fact, it is *possible* for God to share himself with us precisely because he does so covenantally—in the context of a relationship in which he is and always remains the sovereign Lord. To correctly interpret Barth's language of sharing in the divine being, one must understand it within the specific ontological framework that he sets forth here. This is especially important to bear in mind in light of passages such as the following:

> Salvation is fulfillment, the supreme, sufficient, definitive and indestructible fulfillment of being. Salvation is the perfect being [*vollkommenes Sein*] which is not proper to created being as such but is still future. Created being as such needs salvation, but does not have it: it can only look forward to it. To that extent salvation is its *eschaton*. Salvation, fulfillment, perfect being means—and this is what created being does not have in itself—being which has a part in the being of God [*ein Sein in der Teilnahme am Sein Gottes*], from which and to which it is: not a divinized [*nicht ein vergöttlichtes*] being but a being which is hidden in God, and in that sense (distinct from God and secondary) eternal being. Since salvation is not proper to created being as such, it can only come to it, and since it consists in participation in the being of God it can come only from God. The coming of this salvation is the grace of God—using the word in its narrower and most proper sense.[30]

Ignoring Barth's teaching in the first three volumes of the *Church Dogmatics*, one might mistakenly interpret this passage to mean that salvation as human participation in the being of God means something other than the union of divine and human action (and therefore being) in which God's prior action calls forth the human action that faithfully and obediently corresponds to it. On the other hand, if one does not ignore the three previous volumes and the material already presented in this section, but rather interprets this passage in light of them, then it seems nearly impossible to make this mistake. Barth certainly uses the traditional language of participation in the divine being, but he infuses that language with new meaning—his actualistic understanding of divine-human communion. He offers an alternative account in which human participation in God occurs not on the level of a cleansing or transformation of human nature (substantially understood) by either the divine "essence" or "energies," but rather as an event of covenant fellowship in which human beings do not become gods, but rather the human beings they were created to be. Participation in the divine being is "not a divinized being but a being which is hidden in God, and in that sense (distinct from God and secondary) eternal being."[31]

An "Overrealized Eschatology"?

Barth draws an important deduction from the fact that Jesus Christ is himself the event of reconciliation.

> Because He is God He has and exercises the power as this man to suffer for us the consequences of our transgression, the wrath and penalty (*den Zorn und die Strafe*) which necessarily fall on us, and in that way to satisfy Himself in our regard. And again because He is God, He has and exercises the power as this man to be His own partner in our place, the One who in free obedience accepts the ordination of man to salvation which we resist, and in that way satisfies us [*uns genug*], i.e., achieves that which can positively satisfy [*Genügende*] us.[32]

In Jesus Christ, God has made peace between himself and sinful humanity by overcoming sinful humanity and creating a new humanity in its place. Thus, salvation is not a possibility, but a reality, not an opportunity, but the thing itself. God has not merely promised to save humanity. In Jesus Christ, he has fulfilled that promise. Reconciliation is a perfect work. Barth is often criticized at just this point. Has he not gone too far with this line of thought? If Jesus Christ has secured salvation itself, rather than merely its possibility, does that not entirely eliminate the significance of human response?[33] How could anyone reasonably disagree with the charge that Barth's eschatology is "overrealized"?[34]

In order to answer these questions, an important distinction needs to be made. According to Barth, God has saved sinful humanity without its cooperation or consent. God does not ask sinful human beings if they would like to be saved. In Jesus Christ, he just saves them. In Jesus Christ, the salvation of humanity is objective, real, and perfect. This is so entirely apart from how anyone might respond to this fact. Yet Barth also clearly teaches that there is a corresponding subjective counterpart to this objective fact, a point that I have been stressing throughout this study. Jesus Christ is himself both the gospel of the salvation of humanity and the law that summons individuals to realize this truth in their own lives, to be who they are in him. Despite what many of his critics assert, from the beginning of the *Church Dogmatics* to the end, Barth resolutely maintains that there is a difference—indeed a real and important difference—between the accomplishment of salvation in Jesus Christ and the realization of this fact within the lives of those whom he represents. In other words, there is a substantive difference between de jure and de facto participation in Christ. Yet Barth often makes such strong claims about objective participation in Christ that many readers find it difficult to believe that he could possibly have anything else to say. Or if they recognize that he does have more to say, indeed a great deal more, they struggle to know how to take such statements seriously. The solution to this problem lies in the perception that de jure participation in Christ is a teleological reality.

Salvation is not first of all a question posed to humanity. It is a truth proclaimed to humanity. But this truth itself poses a question that demands an answer from humanity. Or, to put it another way, Jesus Christ is the answer to the question of human salvation, and as such poses the further question to humanity: Will you be who you really are? Thus, while our salvation is an accomplished reality in Jesus Christ, not merely a possibility, this does not exclude but includes the fact that this reality awaits its confirmation and fulfillment in the lives of individuals by the power of the Holy Spirit. For Barth, reality is the condition for the possibility of real possibility.

Anticipating the criticisms raised above, Barth writes:

> And what is left to us? . . . In what sense is the history of the acts of God at this center and end our history? Are we not without history? Have we not become mere objects? Have we not lost all responsibility? Are we not reduced to mere spectators? Is not our being deprived of all life or activity? Or does it not lack all significance as our life and activity?[35]

Barth knows that his affirmation of objective participation in Christ leads his critics to raise such questions. Thus he asks, What does it mean to say that "we ourselves are there [i.e., there in and with Jesus Christ] in our being, life and activity?"[36] In other words, What is the nature of objective participation in Christ? The answer, he responds, "is that we ourselves are directly summoned, that we are lifted up, that we are awakened to our own truest being as life and act, that we are set in motion by the fact that in that one man God has made Himself our peacemaker and the giver and gift of our salvation."[37] This does not entail "the extinguishing of our humanity, but its establishment," and this, Barth emphasizes, "is not a small thing, but the greatest of all."[38] Thus, Barth is attempting to turn the tables on his critics by insisting that rather than turning human beings into irrelevant objects, objective participation in Christ actually does the opposite. It creates and establishes them as freely responsible human subjects. Thus, as an elaboration of the meaning of objective participation, Barth writes:

> It is not for us a passive presence as spectators, but our true and highest activation. . . . The genuine being of man as life and activity, the "We with God," is to affirm this, to admit that God is right, to be thankful for it, to accept the promise and the command which it contains, to exist as the community, and responsibly in the community, of those who know that this is all that remains to us, but that it does remain to us and that for all men everything depends upon it coming to pass.[39]

It is not a slip of the pen when Barth writes that "for all men everything depends upon it coming to pass." The objective inclusion of humanity in Jesus Christ is not the end of the story, but the beginning. It is the establishment and anticipation of the end, but not the end itself. The only thing brought to an end in Jesus Christ is sinful humanity. The proper response to grace is not finally silence, but praise. Objective participation is a promise, which demands an unconditional response. Jesus Christ alters the human situation at its most basic level. He does this in order that each and every individual might receive the blessing of life in covenant fellowship with God—the blessing of participation in the divine being. But apart from active participation—apart from the faith, hope, and love that constitute the proper human response to grace—that blessing remains unrealized in those for whom it is accomplished and intended. True humanity is only realized in these obedient human actions. That is why "everything depends upon it coming to pass." Thus, the "existentialism" of *CD* I/1 has not been left behind, but rather given a solid grounding in the objective participation of humanity in Jesus Christ, itself a teleological reality. Barth's theology is not merely the opposite of Rudolf Bultmann's. Bultmann's emphasis on the importance and significance of subjective appropriation and response to the gospel is alive and well here. In Barth's theology, however, that emphasis is located within an objective framework entirely lacking in Bultmann.

"THE GRACE OF GOD IN JESUS CHRIST" (*CD* § 58.1)

The opening section of paragraph fifty-eight is a reflection on "one primary thing": that reconciliation is the free act of God's grace, the free act of the "freest possible subject."[40] Everything in this section is an elaboration on this initial assertion. This is important to recognize because it means that the attack on the Roman Catholic theology of grace that Barth offers here should be read as a defense of this central point. Barth's basic thesis is that Jesus Christ is the sole and "inexhaustible source" of our knowledge of grace because Jesus Christ is himself grace.[41] He is "our wisdom and our righteousness and sanctification and redemption" (1 Cor. 1:30). Therefore grace is alien to its recipients. They receive it, but they do not possess it. It is given to them, but it never comes under their control because Jesus Christ gives himself without giving himself away. In other words, the gift of grace cannot be separated from the giver of grace, because the giver is himself the gift. Grace is the relationship between God and humanity established, maintained, and perfected by and in Jesus Christ. Grace is this active (i.e., "historical") personal relationship.[42]

Simul iustus et peccator

This leads Barth to reaffirm Luther's *simul iustus et peccator* doctrine. "When man is asked concerning his righteousness or holiness or truth, he can only point to his utter lack [*Mangel*] of all these things and then at once point away from himself to his clothing or crowning with all these things, that is, to Jesus Christ."[43] On reflection, many readers would find this statement unsatisfying or perhaps even misanthropic. Why would Barth want to say that human beings are themselves devoid of righteousness, holiness, and truth? After all, is not the covenantal relation established and fulfilled in Jesus Christ a relationship of mutual (divine-human) fellowship and therefore two-sided? And is not the human side of this relationship one of freely spontaneous and faithfully obedient action? And has not Barth already affirmed precisely this? So why would he deny that within this relationship the human partner has a righteousness and holiness of her own? Why does he affirm the *simul iustus et peccator* doctrine?

The preceding quote points to the answers to these questions. Humanity exists only in relationship with Jesus Christ. To think of humanity apart from this relationship is merely to entertain an abstraction. Jesus Christ "clothes" humanity with himself and therefore with righteousness, holiness, and truth. Humanity does not possess these things any more than it possesses Jesus Christ. Yet while it does not possess them, it does receive them, and therefore it is not without them. That is the specific function of the *simul iustus et peccator* doctrine as Barth employs it. Despite appearances, it is not first of all a statement about the sin and righteousness of the Christian. It is rather an affirmation that the source of that righteousness (Jesus Christ) lies outside (*aliena*) the believer. The *simul iustus et peccator* guarantees that Jesus Christ is not merely a step along the way, but the content of salvation itself. Thus, the most basic character of human life in fellowship with God is total, moment-to-moment dependence. Everything that human beings in fellowship with God receive, they must continually receive or else lose.

The Indivisibility of Grace and Interior Renewal

But upon hearing this explanation, many would remain unsatisfied. Is this not still inadequate? Where is the interior renewal, the formation of virtue, character, and habits, the transformation of the soul, the real and inward change that is surely created within the believer?[44] Yes, Jesus Christ is himself our righteousness, it might be asserted, but surely he creates in us a righteousness that is, in one way or another, our own apart from him. If not, then justification and sanctification seem to be a legal fiction—for we, after all, are the ones who are justified and sanctified.

The first thing to point out is that Barth does not respond to this criticism by denying that inward transformation takes place. The transition from sin to obedience, from unbelief to faith, from enmity to love, from hopelessness or misplaced hope to hope in Jesus Christ, indeed from death to life, is as personal and existential a transformation as can take place. Instead, Barth responds by denying the ontology of grace that underlies this argument.

Barth's premise is that grace is not a thing, nor many different kinds of things, but a single acting person. Grace is not detachable from God's action, because grace *is* God's action. It draws forth human response, but it does not create effects that linger in the pious soul apart from God's action. Barth's most penetrating, and finally his only, disagreement with the Roman Catholic divisions of grace (*gratia increata/creata; gratia externa/ interna; gratia actualis/habitualis; gratia medicinalis/elevans; gratia praeveniens/concomitans; gratia operans/cooperans; gratia sufficiens/efficax; gratia christi/Dei; gratia supernaturalis/naturalis*)[45] is not that Roman Catholic teaching finally becomes a "system of fatal preferences,"[46] an inappropriate preoccupation with the second half of these pairs. Nor is it that grace comes to be viewed as a created product, a possession of the soul, a *habitus* separable from the actual operation of grace itself. It is not even that God's action is synthesized with the human action, which cooperates with God's action by free will, both actions therefore being understood as occurring on the same level, mutually limiting and conditioning each other, with God's grace finally being merely preparatory, a *conditio sine qua non*, rather than a "pure *operari*."[47] According to Barth, these mistakes, as well as others, can only arise on the heels of a previous and even more basic mistake, namely, the attempt to divide grace at all.[48]

Grace cannot be divided, because Jesus Christ cannot be divided. But in Barth's view, the attempt is unnecessary anyway. He writes:

> If it is a matter of the grace of the one God and the one Christ, there can be only one grace. We cannot, therefore, split it up into an objective grace which is not as such strong and effective for man but simply comes before him as a possibility, and a subjective grace which, occasioned and pre-pared by the former, is the corresponding reality as it actually comes to man.[49]

Careful attention must be paid to what Barth is and is not saying in this passage. He is not rejecting the distinction between God's action and human response, but rather a specific understanding of the meaning of the objectivity of grace, namely, grace understood as a mere offer or impetus. Against this view, Barth is arguing for a grace "which is subjectively strong and effective in its divine objectivity."[50] Thus, he argues that "it is appar-ent at once that the formula 'God everything and man nothing' as a description of grace is not merely a 'shocking simplification' but complete nonsense."[51] And it is nonsense because the telos of God's reconciliation of humanity in Jesus Christ is the creation of a covenant partner.

> The meaning and purpose of the atonement made in Jesus Christ is that man should not cease to be a subject in relation to God but that he should be maintained as such, or rather—seeing that he has himself surrendered himself as such—that he should be newly created and grounded as such, from above. This creating and grounding of a human subject which is new in relation to God and therefore in itself is, in fact, the event of the atonement made in Jesus Christ. This is what was altered in Him. This is what was accomplished by the grace of God effective and revealed in Him. In Him a new subject was introduced, the true man beside and out-side whom God does not know any other, beside and outside whom there is no other, beside and outside of whom the other being of man, that old being which still continues to break the covenant, can only be a lie, an absurd self-deception, a shadow moving on the wall—the being of that man who has been long since superseded and replaced [*überholt und erledigt*] and who can only imagine that he is man, while in reality he is nothing.[52]

This entire line of thought is only possible (or intelligible for that matter) in light of Barth's Christological anthropology and, specifically, the distinc-tion between objective and subjective participation in Christ. Among other things, that anthropology is enabling Barth to break through and to entirely dispense with the objective-subjective framework upon which the Roman Catholic division of grace is built. In its place, Barth suggests that "the genuinely subjective is already included in the true objective, and will be found in it and not elsewhere."[53] The teleological power of de jure participation in Christ yields not only an alternative to the Roman Catholic understanding of grace, but an alternative anthropology as well. Human "being" is not the possession of self-contained individuals free to accept or reject God's grace. Rather, human being is *enacted* in response to God's grace. In this act, the individual whom Jesus Christ has established as a freely active subject in him embraces this identity and becomes in herself who she is in him.

Thus, Barth's alternative to the Roman Catholic position is not an argument against the reality of God's gracious transformation of human existence. Rather, it is an affirmation that because this transformation has really taken place in Jesus Christ, it will also, and for that reason, really take place in human beings. Barth is not so much denying that grace inwardly transforms the individual to whom it comes as he is affirming that there is nothing more personal or real than the acts in which human beings respond to God's grace. Personal participation in the history of discipleship, the circle of God's action and obedient human response, is the most inward and real event possible to human beings. The Christian community "does not know anything higher or better or more intimate or real than the fact that quite apart from anything that man can contribute to God or become and be in contrast to Him, unreservedly therefore and undeservedly, he can hold fast to God and live by and in this holding fast to Him."[54]

"THE BEING OF HUMANITY IN JESUS CHRIST" (*CD* § 58.2)

Triplex gratia

Jesus Christ, who is himself grace, cannot be divided, and therefore grace cannot be divided. That is the thesis of the material just covered. In the remaining sections of this paragraph, Barth argues that the one grace of Jesus Christ has three aspects. Reconciliation, the fulfillment of the covenant in Jesus Christ, is the accomplishment and revelation of the threefold conversion (*Umkehrung*) of sinful humanity to God, the displacement of the old humanity and the establishment of the new humanity in him. Reconciliation occurs as the event of the justification, sanctification, and calling of humanity in Jesus Christ. These three aspects together constitute the *being* of humanity in him. They define human being because they denote the three aspects of the reconciliation of humanity accomplished in Jesus Christ. Faith, love, and hope are the obedient responses to Jesus Christ that correspond to these three aspects of the objective being of humanity in him, and these responses are the three forms in which this new being is actualized in Christians.[55] In the remainder of this chapter, I will set forth Barth's understanding of these three aspects of grace, and then I will examine their relationships with one another.

Justification

According to Barth, justification is the divine verdict that repudiates, displaces, removes, and pardons the being of sinful humanity and in its place establishes a new and truly human subject who receives the new humanity in faith as an act of pure and obedient gratitude. Justification is the effective sentence that has fallen on Jesus Christ instead of on sinful humanity. This verdict abolishes sinful humanity as such, and in Jesus Christ declares, creates, recognizes, and accepts in its place God's new and faithful covenant partner. Thus, "the being of the new man in the form of faith is man's recognition, acknowledgment and acceptance of this verdict [Urteil], the making of his own subjection to this verdict."[56]

The verdict to which faith subjects itself has "both a negative and a positive meaning and content."[57] On the negative side, Jesus Christ saves sinful humanity by suffering for them "the wrath of God which is the fire of His love."[58] Suffering this end for them, he brings sinful humanity to an end. "In and with the man who was taken down dead on Golgotha man the covenant-breaker is buried and destroyed. He has ceased to be,"[59] and therefore sinful humanity "as such has no future."[60] Furthermore, this verdict justifies not only sinful humanity, but also God himself over against sinful humanity. By dealing with the sinner in this way, "God has vindicated Himself in relation to this man, as He did as Creator in relation to chaos. He could not, and would not, use this man. He could not, and would not, tolerate and have him any longer. He could and would only do away with him."[61] Thus, the divine verdict must also be viewed as "a judicial act [Rechtsakt] in which God has maintained his glory in relation to man."[62]

Turning now to the positive side, justification is a "verdict which recognizes and accepts."[63] Justification is the acknowledgment and proclamation of Jesus Christ as the righteous one, and the acceptance in him of those whom he represents as "not merely innocent but positively righteous."[64] This acceptance is based on Jesus Christ's obedient representation of humanity, his fulfillment of the covenant for them, and the fact that in him sinful humanity has been put to death and replaced by a new humanity.

> In their place Jesus Christ rendered that obedience which is required of the covenant partner of God, and in that way found His good pleasure. He did it by taking to Himself the sins of all men, by suffering as His death the death to which they had fallen a prey, by offering Himself as the sacrifice which had to be made when God vindicated Himself in relation to man,

by choosing to suffer the wrath of God in His own body and the fire of His love in His own soul. It was in that way that He was obedient. It was in that way that He was the righteous One. It was in that way that He was recognized by God—and since He took the place of all, all men in Him.[65]

Jesus Christ's resurrection from the dead is "at once the fulfillment and the proclamation of this positive sentence of God."[66] "This man was brought in with the resurrection of Jesus Christ from the grave."[67] God "willed this man. And what He willed took place. This man came, the man who is righteous for us all, who is our righteousness before God."[68]

Thus, justification is no mere legal fiction. It is a verdict, a "sentence,"[69] a "judicial act."[70] But it is efficacious because it is *God's* verdict. Justification is wholly and utterly transformative, destroying sinful humanity and ushering in a new humanity in its place. Justification is true because it happened in Jesus Christ and he is the measure of all truth. As Barth writes:

> There is no room for any fears that in the justification of man we are dealing only with a verbal action, with a kind of bracketed "as if," as though what is pronounced were not the whole truth about man. Certainly we have to do with a declaring righteous, but it is a declaration about man which is fulfilled and therefore effective in this event, which corresponds to actuality because it creates and therefore reveals the actuality. It is a declaring righteous [*Gerechtsprechung*] which without any reserve can be called a making righteous [*Gerechtmachung*]. Christian faith does not believe in a sentence which is ineffective, or only partly effective. As faith in Jesus Christ who is risen from the dead it believes in a sentence which is absolutely effective, so that man is not merely called righteous before God, but is righteous before God [*der Mensch ein vor Gott Gerechter nicht nur heißt, sondern ist*]. He believes that God has vindicated Himself in relation to man, not partly but wholly, not negatively only but positively, replacing the old man by a new and obedient man.[71]

According to Barth, justification—the replacement of the old human with the new—is an event in Jesus Christ prior to and apart from the faith of those for whom it was accomplished. Christian faith embraces the divine verdict, and in so doing the new humanity which justification ushers in is realized in the lives of individuals. "In the light of this Christian faith itself, as man's subjection to this verdict, can be understood as a form of the being of the new man."[72] Examination of one's own existence invariably reveals that it "contradicts his being in Jesus Christ,"[73] and therefore faith in Jesus Christ means lack of faith in oneself. Since there is nothing within us which serves as confirmation or proof of our righteousness before God, "Christian faith will cling to and find its confidence and support in the divinity of the justifying sentence."[74] Such faith is the gift of the Holy Spirit and the actualization within the Christian of her being as it is in Christ.

Sanctification

In addition to justification, there is a second form of the conversion of humanity to God in Jesus Christ. In justification, God decides "what man really is and is not," and he decides that in Christ each and every person is his child, at peace with him in his kingdom.[75] In Jesus Christ humanity has been placed within God's sphere, within his kingdom. Sanctification is "the all powerful direction of God [*Gottes mächtige Anweisung*] to us to occupy this space, to live in this kingdom."[76] Jesus Christ is God's command to make use of the freedom which is ours as his children. Jesus Christ is our sanctification. He is God's direction, God's command to live as his children. He is not the command to enter into the kingdom of God, but rather the command to live as those who are in it already—to live as those "who have no other place than this."[77] Sanctification is the command "to realize that in Him we are already inside."[78] It is the "claiming of all human life and being and activity by the will of God for the active fulfillment of that will."[79] Jesus Christ is at once the fulfillment of the will of God and the direction to accept this fulfillment in our own lives.

Just as faith responds to the divine verdict of justification, so love responds to the divine direction of sanctification. Just as the first aspect of the new being is actualized in the obedience of faith, its second aspect is actualized in the obedience of love. "The being of man in the form of Christian love consists in the fact that he accepts the divine direction."[80] "In Jesus Christ God has created a final and indestructible fellowship [*endgültige und unzerstörbare Gemeinschaft*] between Himself and all men, between all men and Himself," and Christian love "consists simply in the affirmation of the existence of this fellowship as such, just as faith consists in the affirmation of its foundation."[81] Like faith, love is a free act of pure gratitude, a second form of the new being in Christ.

Vocation

In addition to justification and sanctification, the conversion of humanity to God in Jesus Christ has a third aspect—vocation. The one grace of God in Jesus Christ involves not only the verdict of the Father and the direction of the Son, but also the promise of the Spirit. Like justification and sanctification, vocation is a reality in Jesus Christ, an aspect of the reconciliation of God and humanity in him. No less than faith and love, hope is a form of de facto participation in Christ. In fact, vocation is the telos of justification and sanctification, and therefore "the being of man in Jesus Christ is a being not merely in possession and action but also in expectation."[82] Thus, the new humanity "in its totality is teleologically directed, an eschatological being."[83] Jesus Christ is himself God's promise of humanity's future,

the revelation that "God has in fact a purpose for man in all of this."[84] But
what is the content of this promised future? What is the end toward which
humanity is directed in Christ?

The most distinctive aspect of Barth's answer to this question is his insistence that eternal life is life in action. It is life in union with *God*, not with
"a supreme being with neither life, nor activity, nor history . . . a being with
which man can ultimately be united only in rest or in some kind of passive
enjoyment or adoring contemplation."[85] Therefore, eternal life is an altogether active life.

> If it is the case that man is given a promise for his own future in this as
> yet unrevealed depth of fellowship [*jetzt noch verborgenen Tiefe der
> Gemeinschaft*] with God, it cannot be otherwise than that the content of
> the promise should correspond to the being of God. The fellowship of
> man with God is completed and completes itself as it enters this depth.
> And this complete fellowship, the "eternal" life of man, must consist in
> a future being of man with God as this active ruler.[86]

Barth chooses the word service (*Dienst*) as the leading concept in his description of eternal life precisely because it denotes a life of action: eternal life is
"a being in the service of God."[87] To the extent that the dynamic character of
eternal life is neglected or underplayed in favor of static descriptions—
e.g., "passive enjoyment or adoring contemplation"—it ceases to be a specifically Christian account of life in fellowship with the Lord. Barth is not
wholly opposed to the use of such terms—"We need not be fanatically anti-
mystical"—so long as one understands that to enjoy, contemplate, adore,
and rest in *this* God means to live as his obedient partners within the
covenant, and therefore in active response to this active ruler.[88] In fact, the
historical character of eternal life—its dynamic of lordship and obedience—
guarantees that within this fellowship, and all the way to its depths, the
human person will not "cease to be a man, a creature and as such identical
with himself, the one he now is," and certainly will not "be merged into God
or changed into some quite different being."[89] "The future of man in
covenant with God (in the position and function which he will have in relation to that of God) is to be the partner of God and to live as such."[90]

Therefore, God's call in Jesus Christ is to seize this future even in the present and in so doing to move toward one's future being, indeed toward Jesus
Christ himself—the one in whom this future is already present. Christian
hope is neither wishful thinking nor a promise one makes to one's self,
because Jesus Christ is God's effective promise of eternal life and therefore
hope rests entirely in him. "He Himself as the eternally living God is also
the eternally living man," and as such is "the pledge of what we ourselves
will be."[91] Once again the participation in Christ framework is holding
the argument together: "In the act of Christian hope the objective becomes

subjective. . . . In the act of Christian hope man lives not merely in the factuality of the decision made by God concerning his whole being, but also in the factuality of his own corresponding thoughts and words and works in relation to the service of God."[92] Moreover, de facto participation in Christ is not merely nominal, but real, existentially transformative, and decisively significant.

> Christians do not merely see things differently from others. From God's point of view they are different from others, just as they are different from others in relation to the divine verdict and direction when the Holy Spirit awakens them to faith and love. They do not merely live under the promise, which could be said of all men. They live in and with and by the promise. They seize it. They apprehend it. They conform themselves to it. And therefore in their present life they live as those who belong to the future.[93]

If the promise of a "perfect being" (vollkommenes Sein) in service of Jesus Christ is just that, a promise, then it is a depth of fellowship which is real in Jesus Christ for believers, but is not yet fulfilled in their own lives.[94] And how could it be? If it were already fulfilled in them, then it could not be pledged—it could not be a promise. Thus, if it is not yet fulfilled in them, it is a possibility—a guaranteed possibility to be sure, since it is God's promise, but a possibility nevertheless, the possibility of the realization of this being-in-fellowship in the obedience of faith, love, and hope. When, by the power of the Holy Spirit, faith, love, and hope are offered as responses to the divine verdict, direction, and promise, that which is objectively true becomes subjectively true.

CONCLUDING OBSERVATION

We are now in a position to make an important concluding observation regarding the relationship between the various aspects of the one grace of God. Justification, sanctification, and vocation are not loci developed independently or alongside Christology, but rather derive wholly from Christology. Or, even more strongly, they are events in Jesus Christ. "What is said about Jesus Christ Himself, the Christological propositions as such, are constitutive, essential, necessary and central in the Christian doctrine of reconciliation."[95] Jesus Christ is the active subject of reconciliation, not merely a means or predicate of its happening, and thus justification, sanctification, and calling pertain to each and every individual only because each and every individual has Jesus Christ as his or her representative and head.

Thus, since the new humanity is inseparable from Jesus Christ who is himself the new human, the realization of the new being in faith, love, and hope is at every point a being in relationship with the person of Jesus Christ, and thus a being in union with him. Faith, love, and hope are the modes of this union, responses that correspond to the justification, sanctification, and calling which have been accomplished in him. As Barth writes, "Christians exist in Him. In practice this is the only thing that we can call their peculiar being."[96]

On this construal of the matter, the question of which is more basic—union with Christ, on the one hand, or justification, sanctification, and vocation on the other—does not arise. And it does not arise because the objective being of humanity in Jesus Christ just is the verdict, direction, and promise given in each of these three aspects of reconciliation. In the relationship of Jesus Christ to humanity, *he* is more basic than they because he is their Savior and Representative while they are saved and represented. Thus, the objective inclusion of humanity in Jesus Christ is more basic than the obedient responses to Jesus Christ because the latter are the realization of the telos established in the former, and for that reason justification, sanctification, and calling are more basic than faith, love, and hope, which receive and affirm them. But that is just another way of saying that objective participation in Christ is more basic than subjective participation in Christ. If one wanted to press the question, it could be made more precise by asking: Which is more basic—*objective* union with Christ, on the one hand, or justification, sanctification, and vocation on the other? The question immediately answers itself, however, because the objective being of humanity in Jesus Christ *is* justification, sanctification, and vocation. Those are the three aspects of the new being of humanity created in him. The new being is a being under the verdict, direction, and promise of God. When looked at in this way, Barth's famous statement that the *articulus stantis et cadentis ecclesiae* is not the doctrine of justification, but the confession of Jesus Christ, is not as iconoclastic as it first appears.[97] His point is simply that justification is only one of the three aspects of the new humanity which Jesus Christ is.

5

CHRISTOLOGY AS THE KEY
TO THE WHOLE

At the beginning of his brief introduction to Barth's theology, Colm O'Grady makes the following remark: "We will not understand Barth until we understand the way or form in which his thought runs. One thinks immediately of his actualistic thought-form with which he wishes to exclude all staticism."[1] Then, a few pages later, as an example of Barth's actualism, O'Grady quotes the following passage from *CD* IV/2:

> From the very first we have understood and interpreted the doctrine of the incarnation . . . in historical terms, as an *operatio* between God and man, fulfilled in Jesus Christ as a union of God with man. We have represented the existence of Jesus Christ as His being in His act. . . . We have left no place for anything static at the broad center of the traditional doctrine of the person of Christ—its development of the concepts of *unio*, *communio* and *communicatio*—or in the traditional doctrine of the two states. . . . But—thinking and speaking in pure concepts of movement— we have re-translated that whole phenomenology into the sphere of a history. And we have done this because originally the theme of it is not a phenomenon, or a complex of phenomena, but a history.[2]

In the library copy of O'Grady's book that I am using, just beside Barth's quote someone has simply written"?" It is not an uncommon response to reading Barth. And yet O'Grady's observation is sound, especially as it pertains to Barth's Christology. Without a firm grasp on Barth's actualism, his Christology cannot possibly be understood. For the dynamic, active, historical, and covenantal character of Barth's Christology is what sets it apart from all others and is its most distinguishing feature. While Barth engages in sustained conversation with the history of the church's thinking about Jesus Christ, and while he is especially sympathetic to the Christology of Reformed Orthodoxy, the more one reads this material, the more one is struck by the sheer innovation, and indeed singularity, of Barth's Christology.

In this final chapter, I will treat the section that Barth referred to as "the decisive center" (*entscheidendend Mitte*)[3] of his Christology.[4] I will then make an observation concerning the section in paragraph sixty-six titled "The Holy One and the Saints,"[5] in which the theme of participation in Christ takes center stage. I will conclude with an examination of the section titled "The Goal of Vocation" in paragraph seventy-one of *CD* IV/3, in which Barth treats union with Christ.[6] This final section draws together, clarifies, and accentuates many of the leading ideas in this study as a whole.

THE "DECISIVE CENTER" OF BARTH'S CHRISTOLOGY (*CD* § 64.2)

The string of quotes cited by O'Grady, to which I referred above, is located in the Christology paragraph which opens *CD* IV/2. In the course of his presentation, and just prior to his treatment of what the Reformed and Lutheran theologians of the seventeenth century called the *communicatio operationum*—"the cooperation of the two natures to specific ends or results"—Barth paused to assess the Christology that he had set forth.[7] "What is it, then, that we have done?" In addition to the important sentences cited by O'Grady, Barth makes the following observation:

> We have "actualized" the doctrine of the incarnation, i.e., we have used the main traditional concepts, *unio*, *communio*, and *communicatio*, as concentrically related terms to describe one and the same ongoing process. We have stated it all (including the Chalcedonian definition, which is so important in dogmatic history, and rightly became normative) in the form of a denotation and description of a single event [*eines einzigen Ereignisses*]. We have taken it that the reality of Jesus Christ, which is the theme of Christology, is identical with this event, and this event with the reality of Jesus Christ.[8]

Barth's awareness of his decisive break with traditional construals of the person and work of Christ led him to make the following remark concerning classical Christology:

> The distinguishing feature of this whole conception is the calm both in the description of the divine-human being of Jesus Christ and in the doctrine of the two states. And it was a conception common not only to the traditional Christology of the Middle Ages and the Early Church, but also to that of both Lutherans and Reformed. We have given a relative preference to the Reformed because of its persistent and certainly instructive and pregnant centering on the decisive concept of the *unio hypostatica*. But there can be no doubt that in our departure from this whole conception we have left even Reformed Christology far behind. We cannot expect to be praised for our "orthodoxy" from any quarter.[9]

Barth anticipated that his Christology in general, and his reversal of the traditional ordering of being and act in particular, would generate criticism from both conservative and liberal theologians alike—the former for his jettisoning of familiar modes of thought and the latter for his remaining too closely tied to traditional Christology. But in addition to its soundness, he also anticipated that he would be challenged regarding its very possibility.

> The question of possibility is a serious one. For the transposition undoubtedly means a disturbance of the relatively perspicuous pragmatics of the older conception. And it involves logical difficulties which, if they were not really overcome, were carefully concealed in the latter. How can a being be interpreted as an act, or an act as a being? How can God, or man, or both in their unity in Jesus Christ, be understood as history?[10]

Characteristically, Barth offers no neutral justification for his procedure. He simply states that an adequate description of Jesus Christ demands it: "The questions of legitimacy and possibility are decided by that of necessity."[11] However, he then adds that the *unio hypostatica* demands it. This is a terribly important point.

Jesus Christ is both God and human. The older Christologies affirmed this, and according to Barth any subsequent theology that wishes to be Christian must likewise affirm it. But in Barth's view the common flaw in the older Christologies is their description of the hypostatic union in static rather than active-historical terms. Jesus Christ is both God and human, Barth asserts, but he is so dynamically and historically as an event, not statically as the joining of two independently existing substances.

> For what is the meaning, in this answer, of the little word "and"? This "and" tells us who He is. But is there any standpoint from which we can see and expound it as the description of an immobile and rigid contiguity and fusion of two elements? Certainly, the word speaks of a union [*Vereinigung*]. But it is a union in which there can be neither mixture nor change, division nor separation. The being of Jesus Christ consists in this union. "Union"? To say this is already to suggest an act, or movement. . . . On what ground, *quo iure*, is the distinction made between *unitio* and *unio*, which necessarily results in *unio* acquiring the sense of *unitas* and denoting a static and non-actual twofold being, with inevitable consequences for the interpretation of *communio* and *communicatio*? Can we say "Jesus Christ," and therefore "God and man," "Creator and creature," without making it clear that we are speaking of the One who exists in this way only in the act of God, and therefore the occurrence of this history? Can we see what He became in this act, "God and man," but ignore—or leave behind as a mere presupposition—the act in which He became it, and therefore His becoming? Can we say *Verbum caro* but conceal, or give no emphasis to, the *factum est*?[12]

Therefore, while "the transposition of the static statements of older dogmatics is undoubtedly an innovation [*Neuerung*]," Barth regarded it as nothing less than the necessary form of an adequate witness to the fact that Jesus Christ is *alive*.[13] In that sense, Barth's actualistic construal of the *unio hypostatica* is an attempt to avoid idolatry, an attempt to bear witness to living reality of the living Lord Jesus Christ.

Barth's Christology is not the outworking of a commitment to a preconceived actualistic ontology, but rather an attempt to offer a fitting description of the living Lord Jesus Christ himself, as attested by Holy Scripture. Barth asks, "Does not everything depend on our doing justice to the living Jesus Christ? But, at root, what is the life of Jesus Christ but the act in which God becomes very God and very man, positing Himself in this being? What is it but the work of this conjunction?"[14] Since Jesus Christ is himself the event of this history, historical thinking—in the Barthian sense—is the fitting mode of description. "There can be only a historical thinking, for which each factor has its own distinctive character. The divine and the human work together. But even in their common working they are not interchangeable. The divine is still above and the human below. Their relationship is one of genuine action."[15] Jesus Christ is "the common *actualization* of divine and human essence."[16] The *being* of Jesus Christ as divine and human is in the specifically coordinated event of this union. Thus, Barth concludes that Jesus Christ "is in this *operatio*, this event. This is the new form which we have given to Christology in our present understanding and development of it."[17] But why should this be such an important point? Why draw such attention to it? And what does it have to do with the theme of participation in Christ?

Simply put, the Christology is the key to the whole volume, and covenant-historical thinking is the key to the Christology. All of the contents of *CD* IV/2, including the material on sanctification, the church, and Christian love, receive their decisive impetus from, and rest entirely upon, the opening Christology. Moreover, and of special importance to this study, the category within which Barth explores the history of Jesus Christ—his one person and work—is the "mutual participation" of the human essence in the divine and the divine essence in the human. The event of this mutual participation is the event of his person—*unio hypostatica*—and the accomplishment of the exaltation of humanity. The participation of humanity in Jesus Christ occurs objectively within this history of mutual participation and subjectively in a way that corresponds to this history.[18] In the preface to *CD* IV/2, Barth offers the reader nothing less than a hermeneutical rule for reading the work as a whole. "The Christological section," he writes:

> stands at the head and contains the whole *in nuce*, speaking as it does of the humanity of Jesus Christ. I cannot advise anyone to skip it either as a

whole or in part in order to rush on as quickly as possible to what is said about sanctification, etc. *For it is there—and this is true of every aspect—that the decisions are made.* There is no legitimate way to an understanding of the Christian life than that which we enter there. As I see it, it is by the extent to which I have correctly described this that the book is to be judged.[19]

The key decisions are made in the Christology paragraph. The following four paragraphs proceed from this source and are nourished by it at every point. "The problem of reconciled humanity, like that of the reconciling God, has to be based in Christology, and can be legitimately posed and developed and answered only on this basis."[20] The actualism of Barth's Christology makes itself felt in a thoroughly actualistic construal of the believer's participation in Christ.[21]

An Orderly Fellowship

As God condescends and humbles Himself to man and becomes man, man himself is exalted, not as God or like God, but to God, being placed at His side, not in identity, but in true fellowship with Him, and becoming a new man in this exaltation and fellowship [*Erhöhung und Gemeinschaft*].[22]

At the heart of the divine-human communion is an irreducible distinction that will never be overcome because Jesus Christ will always be who he is. The hypostatic union itself is an event of lordship and obedience, the perfect coordination of two distinct sets of actions, divine and human, which are never confused with each other.

This two-sided participation [*Dieses beiderseitige Teilnehmen und Teil-haben*], and therefore the union of the two natures in Him, arises and consists, therefore, from Him. Hence it is "from above to below," and only then (as we have seen, in a way which is characteristically different) "from below to above." It is two-sided, but in this sequence, and in the differentiated two-sidedness which this and the difference of the two natures involves. . . . [I]t is not itself a unity [*Einheit*], but a union [*Vereinigung*] in that two-sided participation, the *communio naturarum*. In the one Subject Jesus Christ divine and human essence is united, but it is not one and the same.[23]

The participation of His divine in His human essence is not the same as that of His human in His divine. . . . The determination of His divine essence is *to* His human, and the determination of His human essence *from* His divine. . . . This means that the word mutual [*beiderseitig*] cannot be understood in the sense of interchangeable [*wechselseitig*]. The relationship between the two is not reversible [*umkehrbar*]. That which takes place between them is not cyclic. Each has its own role. . . . What we have here is a real history. It takes place both from above to below and also from below to above. But it takes place from above to below first, and only then from below to above. In it is the self-humiliated Son of God who is also exalted man. He Himself is always the Subject of this history. It is not merely because they are different by definition, but because they have a different relationship to this Subject, that the divine and human essence bear a different character in their mutual participation.[24]

Since the exaltation of humanity is a gift of grace, it must take this differentiated form.

The presence of this distinction, however, does not mean that the mutual participation is merely partial on each side. Rather, each participates totally in the other:

> There is no element of human essence which is unaffected by, or excluded from, its existence in and with the Son of God, and therefore from union with, and participation in, this divine essence. Similarly, there is no element of His divine essence which the Son of God, existing in human essence, withdraws from union with it and participation in it.[25]

In the one person Jesus Christ, the Son of God takes to himself everything that belongs to human beings as covenant-breakers. In so doing, and simultaneously, he becomes the man who receives his being in response to this act of grace, the man whose "being in this exaltation can consist only in an action of the most profound human thankfulness."[26] Thus, the self-offering and humiliation of the Son of God is total as this man, and the grateful response of obedience of the Son of Man is correspondingly total. "The mystery of the incarnation consists in the fact that Jesus Christ is in a real simultaneity of genuinely divine and human essence, and that it is on this presupposition that the mutual participation is also genuine."[27]

Barth elaborates this mutual participation under three headings: *communicatio idiomatum* (the impartation of the divine essence to the human and vice versa); *communicatio gratiarum* (that which is specifically addressed to the human essence in this impartation); and *communicatio operationum* (the common actualization of these two essences). Throughout this discussion, Barth is primarily concerned to affirm that the Son of God is the Lord of the union of his divine and human natures. In fact, the whole presentation is an unfolding of the implications of this point within each of these three areas.

> The indispensable closer definition of this mutual participation must be this. The Son of God is the acting Subject who takes the initiative in this event, and not either His divine or His human essence. . . . He Himself grasps and has and maintains the leadership in what His divine essence is and means for His human, and His human for His divine,

in their mutual participation. He is the norm and limit and criterion in this happening.[28]

This line of argument is an intentional continuation of the trajectory established by traditional Reformed Christology over against the Christology of the Lutherans.

Barth's Christology: Its Reformed Sympathies

In Barth's view, the Lutherans and Reformed were both Chalcedonian, yet the primary emphasis of the Reformed was on the *unio hypostatica*, and therefore the *person* of the union, whereas the Lutheran "interest was not so much in this concept as in the resultant *communio naturarum* and its consequences."[29] The Lutherans were intent on showing that "the divine triumph over the distinction and antithesis between God and man took place directly, and is a fact, in the humanity of Jesus Christ," and therefore on showing that "the Godhead can be seen and grasped and experienced and known directly in the humanity of Jesus Christ."[30] For their part, the Reformed rejected the idea of a direct *communio naturarum*, affirming instead an indirect union of the two natures in the person of the Son, their aim being to guard against the dedivinization of God or the divinization of the human being. Barth's reason for siding with the Reformed is clear. In the first chapter of this study, I showed that revelation occurs indirectly, not directly. At the other end of the *Church Dogmatics*, Barth remained committed to that point. In the meantime, however, he developed the additional, albeit related, conviction that the being of Jesus Christ is his history, and he considered the older Reformed emphasis on the *unio hypostatica* to be a witness to that very point. In Barth's view, the Lutherans denied this crucial insight by looking away from the person of Jesus Christ himself and instead focusing "on the equations which result from" the direct perichoresis of the two natures, i.e., the divinization of his humanity as such.[31] According to Barth, the Reformed rejection of the Lutheran position should not be attributed to "a barren intellectual zeal for the axiom: *finitum non capax infiniti*," but rather to "a zeal for the sovereignty of the Subject acting in free grace in the incarnation."[32] Thus, Barth's conception of the *unio hypostatica* as an event always grounded in the action of the Son of God is an extension of the Reformed emphasis on the sovereignty of the divine Subject of the incarnation into the description of the mode of union itself.[33] While the Reformed theologians were unable to fully realize the inherent power of their dynamic Christology because of their commitment to a traditional ontology, Barth jettisoned that ontology in an attempt to allow his thinking to be shaped entirely by the hypostatic union itself.

Since this very rich section cannot be examined exhaustively, I will conclude by focusing on two important points. The first pertains to the Lutheran emphasis on the divinization of Jesus Christ's humanity, which Barth refers to as "a kind of remote effect of the theology of the Eastern Church."[34] The second concerns the question of the identity of the subject of the incarnation.

Barth's Rejection of Deification

Barth rejects deification repeatedly throughout this material. Yet he does so for a variety of reasons. An analysis of the various contexts in which he criticizes deification reveals that he rejects it for five primary reasons.[35]

The first is simply a concern to avoid Docetism. Speaking of the flesh of Jesus Christ as the temple of God, Barth writes, "Do we have to deify this temple, this dwelling as such, in order that the dwelling of the Godhead in it may be a real one? If it is deified, does it not cease to be His temple? Or, to abandon the metaphor, does not a deified human essence cease to be our human essence?"[36] In Barth's view, the deification of Jesus' human nature necessarily means its transformation into something other than human nature.

Secondly, Barth sees in deification a synergism which denies the sovereignty of God's grace. Consider the following passage:

> For all their reciprocity the two elements in this happening have a different character. The one, as the essence of the Son of God, is wholly that which gives. The other, exalted to existence and actuality only in and by Him, is wholly that which receives. . . . His exaltation as the Son of Man is not the divinization of His human essence. It means that, unchanged as such, it is set in perfect fellowship with the divine essence.[37]

According to Barth, deification either implies or endorses the false idea that the efficacy of God's grace is dependent on human cooperation.

Barth's third reason for rejecting deification is related to the second reason. In Barth's view, a traditional substantialist ontology undermines Jesus Christ's living and active identity by obscuring his historicity. To the extent that deification focuses primarily on the *effect* of the direct penetration of Jesus' flesh by the divine nature, the deification of his human nature as such, it looks away from the living Jesus Christ himself.

> Did the representatives of this view really look openly and directly at Jesus Christ in their thinking? Did they follow through this history? Or did they look only at the given happening as such, the victory which took place in the history, looking away from the event of the divine giving and

human receiving to what is given to the human essence of Jesus Christ in this event, to a status mediated to Him in this event? . . . [T]he human-ity of Jesus Christ as conceived in this way is one long abstraction: abstracted, that is, from the history to which we cannot even for a moment cease to cling if we are to see and think and confess "Jesus Christ." . . . The recognition of Jesus Christ as true salvation and saving truth is not really strengthened, as intended, by the theory of a diviniza-tion of His human essence, but weakened and even jeopardized com-pletely. This is one reason why we have no option but to reject it.[38]

Barth rejects the idea of a *"gratia habitualis* imparted to the human nature of Jesus Christ by infusion" for exactly the same reason.[39] This idea arises only if one looks away from the history in which Jesus Christ has his being to a supposed fact of that history. "*Habitus* comes from *habere*," Barth writes:

and therefore denotes possession. But grace is divine giving and human receiving. It can be "had" only in the course of this history. . . . We can-not look away from the event in which this receiving takes place. We can only look to the event in which it does also take place. There can be no question, then, of a *habitus* proper to the human essence of Jesus Christ. . . . We ourselves must be at great pains to guard against [this] aberration.[40]

Barth rejects the idea that the human nature of Jesus Christ received "a transferred condition [*übermittelte Zuständlichkeit*]," the very heart of the idea of deification, because with the humanity of Jesus Christ "it is all a his-tory."[41] Jesus Christ receives "no permanent state of blessing."[42] His exis-tence is "something new and specific at every step."[43] The continuity of his identity is located neither in a permanent endowment of habitual grace nor in a general and self-identical human nature, but rather in "the fact that He is always the same elect man confronted and surrounded and fulfilled by the same electing grace of God."[44]

Barth's fourth reason for rejecting deification is that he thinks it estab-lishes a trajectory that has as its logical conclusion the superfluity of Jesus Christ himself. To the extent that the deification of the flesh of the Son of God is regarded as a means to the goal of the deification of human beings, Jesus Christ recedes into the background. He performs a necessary role, but on performing it he loses his place of central significance. The theology of deification, in Barth's view, opens the door to the general deification of humanity apart from Jesus Christ. By emphasizing the central and perma-nent significance of the hypostatic union, Barth aims to forestall this pos-sibility by attacking its theological foundation.

But when it speaks of a divinization of human essence in Jesus Christ, and when this divinization of the flesh of Jesus Christ is understood as the supreme and final and proper meaning and purpose of the incarnation—even to the point of worshiping it—a highly equivocal situation is created. . . . For after all, is not the humanity of Jesus Christ, by definition, that of all men? And even if it is said only of Him, does not this mean that the essence of all men, human essence as such, is capable of divinization? If it can be said in relation to Him, why not to all men? But this means that in Christology a door is left wide open, not this time by a secular philosophy which has entered in with subtlety, but in fulfillment of the strictest theological discussion and ostensibly from the very heart of the Christian faith. And through this door it is basically free for anyone to wander right away from Christology. Who is to prevent him?[45]

According to Barth, while Luther and the Lutherans of the sixteenth and seventeenth centuries certainly never envisioned the transition from their Christology to the divinity of humanity as a whole and as such, when this occurred in "the wonderful flower of German Idealism," it was not unrelated to the Christology that had been dominant in Germany for the previous two hundred years.[46]

Luther and the older Lutherans did in fact compromise—at a most crucial point—the irreversibility of the relationship between God and man, long before the message of the Church was similarly affected by a secular human self-understanding which drew its nourishment from a very different quarter. . . . It was also not an accident that the opposition to this tendency which arose about 1920 came from the Reformed side.[47]

Whereas Barth's first four reasons for rejecting deification are defensive in orientation, his fifth reason is positive, as we shall now see.

Barth's Alternative to Deification

I have argued throughout this study that Barth rejects deification not because he thinks it hopelessly off-base, but because he thinks it provides an inadequate answer to a legitimate question. Given the fact that Barth so often rejects deification, it would be easy to draw the conclusion that he dismisses its basic concern as such. He does not: "We do not fail to appreciate the attraction of the particular Lutheran interest in the *communio naturarum,* nor do we wish to ignore the concern which underlies it."[48] Since, as we have already seen, Barth regards the Lutheran interest as a "remote effect of the theology of the Eastern Church," it may be concluded that he views the theology of deification as it emerged in the Eastern Church in the same way.[49] This observation gains further confirmation when he writes, "We cannot keep our distance from at least the intention of this *theologoumenon*, which is so closely akin to the distinctive Eastern Christology and soteriology of the Greek fathers. . . . But when all this has been said, it has also to be perceived and said that this intention cannot be executed *as attempted along these lines.*"[50]

According to Barth, the Reformed correctly rejected the Lutheran understanding of the *communio naturarum*. Their perception of its error was sound, and their refusal to follow its development was prudent. Yet staggered and horrified as they were by it, they simply "gave up the whole problem."[51] "Their reaction," Barth writes, "was much too negative."[52] Barth agrees that "faced with a choice between the existing Lutheran answer and the existing Reformed rejection of the problem, we can only decide that the Reformed chose the better part."[53] Yet he immediately adds that "the question still remains whether the dilemma cannot be evaded. Do we really have to make a choice between these two possibilities?"[54] Barth is convinced that the Lutherans were addressing a problem legitimately posed by Scripture—the exaltation of humanity in the person of Jesus Christ—and therefore rather than simply rejecting the problem as the Reformed did, he seeks to offer a satisfying answer to it. Yet inasmuch as Barth's solution is grounded in the hypostatic union, in Jesus Christ himself, and not in an abstract interest in the effects of that union on his human nature, Barth's answer is distinctly Reformed. So what is Barth's solution? How does he attempt, as he puts it, "to rescue the question from the impasse"?[55]

Recall that the primary subject matter of this paragraph is the exaltation of the Son of Man and humanity in him. Throughout his presentation, in mostly indirect, but also occasionally in direct statements, Barth prepares the reader to expect the answer that he finally gives to the question of the meaning of this exaltation. But he does not fully offer that answer until some ninety pages into this densely packed paragraph. With almost maddening patience and thoroughness, Barth circles this central matter, clarifying exactly where he stands on numerous attendant issues. So when he finally does arrive at his answer, it is close to impossible to miss:

> What the grace of His origin does involve and effect, with supreme necessity and power, is the exaltation of His human essence. Exaltation to what? To that harmony with the divine will, that service of the divine act, that correspondence to the divine grace, that state of thankfulness, which is the only possibility in view of the fact that this man is determined by the divine will and act and grace alone.[56]

The exaltation of humanity in Jesus Christ is "human essence as determined wholly and utterly, from the very outset and in every part, by the electing grace of God."[57] To be human is to live one's life in correspondence with election. More specifically, Jesus Christ is the history of this human response to the divine election. "It is genuinely human in the deepest sense to live by the electing grace of God addressed to man. This is how Jesus Christ lives as the Son of Man."[58] To be exalted is to be truly human, not to be deified. Exaltation is elevation to the freedom of obedience.

In Barth's view, the Lutheran and Orthodox answer says too much. Their intention is laudable, but ironically the net effect of their insistence on the deification of humanity is the denial of the true glory of divine-human communion—the glory of the electing grace of God and the freely offered response of grateful human obedience. Such obedience demands that the "confrontation" between divine and human essence never be over-come, the very thing which deification affirms.[59] Jesus Christ's life is the history of the harmony of this confrontation. "The Son of Man exists only in His identity with the Son of God, and His human essence only in its con-frontation with His divine. Its determination by the electing grace of God is not only its first but also its last and total and exclusive determination."[60] Apart from this confrontation there could be no lordship and obedience, and therefore no exaltation of humanity. Very simply, and almost poignantly, when referring to the deification of Jesus' flesh, Barth writes, "It is hard to see where this necessity arises. It is hard to see why its total and exclusive determination by the grace of God is not enough. It is hard to see why this should not be the absolute distinction and empowering which has come in it to the one Son of Man who is also and primarily the Son of God."[61] What humanity needs, according to Barth, is not deification, but freedom. If "it is genuinely human in the deepest sense to live by the electing grace of God in man," and if this is how Jesus Christ lives as the Son of Man, then it is unwise to wish for anything more.[62] Anything more would, in fact, be less because it would not be fellowship with this God who, thankfully, always remains Lord of his covenant.

The Subject of the Incarnation

My second and final observation about this material concerns the desig-nation of the subject of the incarnation. Who is the subject of the incarna-tion? In other words, Who is the source and ground of the actions of the one person Jesus Christ? From whence do the actions of this one person originate? This is a more difficult question than it first appears. Consider the following statements:

1. "It is primarily and properly this human subject [*dieses menschliche Subjekt*], who, as the object of the free and liberating grace of God, cannot be only an object in the event of atonement, but also becomes an active subject."[63]

2. "The subject Jesus Christ [*Das Subjekt Jesus Christus*] is this history."[64]

3. "He, God the Son, in his divine essence is its active subject" (*Er, Gott der Sohn, in seinem göttlichen Wesen ist das in ihr handelnde Subjekt*).[65]

Thus, according to Barth, the subject of the history in which Jesus Christ has his being is: (1) the man Jesus; (2) Jesus Christ in his divine-human unity; (3) the Son of God. So which is it? And why does it matter?

Barth is not as clear as he should have been in sorting through this question as well as others linked to it. He did not always follow the logic of his decision to "historicize" the incarnation through to the very end, nor did he devise a uniform and fully adequate terminology for expressing what he wanted to say about Jesus Christ. Given the groundbreaking nature of what he was trying to accomplish, that is perhaps understandable. For while Barth broadly operated within the framework of a "two-natures" Christology, he was determined to bring the content of terms such as "nature," "person," and "union" into greater coherence with the living history of Jesus Christ's "active person" (*wirkenden Person*) and "his personal work" (*persönlichen Werkes*).[66] And this endeavor led to large-scale revision and reconceptualization of traditional patterns of Christological description. Still, the main lines of his position can be sorted out. Let us consider the first option.

I have argued throughout this study that Barth's doctrine of election and his Christology do not smother genuine human action, but ground and elicit it. This could certainly not be the case if there is *no sense at all* in which Jesus Christ is a human subject. If Jesus Christ is not a genuinely human subject, then how can we be? The question is, what kind of human subject are we talking about here? Barth is clear that the man Jesus Christ exists only in the person of the Word (*enhypostasis*) and not independently (*anhypostasis*). "As a man, therefore, He exists directly in and with the one God in the mode of existence of His eternal Son and Logos—not otherwise or apart from this mode . . . not autonomously, as would be the case if that with which God united Himself were a *homo* and not *humanitas*."[67] Barth is no adoptionist. "There are not two existing side by side or even within one another. There is only the one God the Son, and no one and nothing either alongside or even in Him. But this One exists, not only in His divine, but also in human being and essence, in our nature and kind."[68] Or, as he vividly puts it, "A predicate cannot be properly seen and understood and portrayed without its subject. But in itself and as such the humanity of Jesus Christ is a predicate without a subject."[69] Jesus Christ is a human being, an acting human agent, inasmuch as he is *responsive* to the actions of God. His human actions do not originate with his humanity but happen humanly as he responds to the actions of God. That is what Barth is affirming when he says that the man Jesus is a human subject. The one person Jesus Christ is the event of the confrontation of the Son of God and Son of Man, the event of this history. Jesus Christ is the man he is wholly within this history, but

within it, and in response to the will of God, he is fully human—a fully obedient and therefore human subject. Nevertheless, his human actions do not
originate independently, but always in response to the divine action toward
him. Thus, once qualified, the first option in our list may be ruled out.

Of the final two options, is it not by now clear that the acting subject of
this history is Jesus Christ in his divine-human unity? Barth has gone to
great lengths to think of Jesus Christ faithfully by thinking of him historically rather than statically, concretely rather than abstractly, and therefore
by focusing on the hypostatic union and not on that which takes place in
the human nature in isolation. Therefore, would not designating the Son
of God—and not Jesus Christ in his divine-human unity—as the acting
subject of the incarnation sever his identity? Would it not destroy the singularity of his person?

The answer to this line of questioning is that the Son of God *abstractly
considered*—i.e., considered apart from the history of Jesus Christ—definitely is not the acting subject of the incarnation. But the Son of God is not
who he is in abstraction. The Son of God is who he is in the assumption of
human flesh, in the event of this one history. And an examination of the
content of this history as one of divine lordship and human obedience
reveals that the Son of God, and not the "God-man," is the acting subject
of the incarnation. Admittedly, this is a somewhat fine distinction, but the
point is important, so I will restate it.

Recall the question being asked: Where do the actions of this one person originate? From what source do they proceed? Jesus Christ is one person—the event of the one history of the Son's assumption of human flesh.
He is fully human and fully divine, and therefore he acts both humanly
and divinely. Yet *because* this is the case, because the hypostatic union can
only be depicted actively, as an event, Barth will not speak of Jesus Christ
as "the God-man (θεάνθρωπος)."[70] He admits that the term is "possible
and tempting," but he avoids it because "it obliterates the historicity of the
subject."[71] According to Barth, "the word God-man obscures again the
event, the *novum* of the act of God, in which Jesus Christ actualizes Himself and is actual."[72] Even more specifically, the term obscures the fact that
the history is one of free divine lordship and correspondingly free human
obedience. God, not the human Jesus, "maintains the initiative in this
event."[73] It is "the Son of God as the subject of the incarnation who creates
and bears and maintains the *communio naturarum*."[74] Barth makes this
point clearly and forcefully in the following passage:

> According to this concept [i.e., mutual participation], they [i.e., the divine
> and human essences] are not united in the Son of God, who is of divine
> essence and assumed human, like two planks lashed or glued together—
> to use an image which often occurs in older polemics—as if each retained

its separate identity in this union and the two remained mutually alien in a neutral proximity. The truth is rather that *in the Son of God, and therefore by the divine Subject, united in His act,* each of the two natures, without being either destroyed or altered, acquires and has its own determination. By and in Him the divine acquires a determination to the human, and the human a determination from the divine. The Son of God takes and has a part in the human essence assumed by Him by giving this a part in His divine essence. And the human essence assumed by Him takes and has a part in His divine by receiving this from Him. The indispensable closer definition of this mutual participation must be this. The Son of God is the acting Subject who takes the initiative in this event, and not either His divine or His human essence.[75]

That is why Barth is convinced that so much rests on this point. Jesus Christ is a single person, but Barth defines the *unio personalis*, the *unio hypostatica*, as an event, as a history. And within this history, there is a very definite order: the divine always gives and the human always receives responsively. Thus, the Son of God maintains the initiative in this event, and in that sense is the sole subject of the incarnation.[76] He is the source and ground of the action that elicits the response in which Jesus Christ is the man he is. It is not simply a matter of historical curiosity whether Barth's Christology is more "Alexandrian" or "Antiochene"—i.e., whether the Son of God is the sole acting subject of the incarnation (God *as* man) or two cooperating subjects (the Son of God and the man Jesus). The question is not so much a comparison of whether Barth's Christology is more like that of Cyril or of Nestorius. It is rather a referendum on the theology of Pelagius and its variants. If the person Jesus Christ is the history of the mutual participation of divine and human essences, then to say that the human essence only *is* in response to God's prior action, to say that the man Jesus would not *be* at all apart from the acts in which he is united in response to the Son of God who unites himself with this man, is to affirm that the man Jesus owes his entire existence to the election of divine grace. And that is exactly what Barth says: "He derives exclusively from this will and this act. . . . The grace of God alone is His origin and determination. . . . This man is none other than the Son."[77]

George Hunsinger has helpfully pointed out that Barth speaks in the "idioms" of both Antioch and Alexandria.[78] Importantly, every single one of the former cases of which I am aware is simply a witness to the fact that Jesus Christ is fully human, that within the event of his history he acts as a man in response to God's grace. Yet if a defining feature of Antiochene Christological thinking is judged to be the affirmation that Jesus Christ is a fully and independently acting human subject, then in that important sense there is nothing Antiochene about Barth's Christology, whether in *CD* IV/2 or elsewhere.[79] As Barth writes:

The divine act of humility fulfilled in the Son is the only ground of this happening and being. On this ground the unity achieved in this history has to be described, not as two sided, but as founded and consisting absolutely and exclusively in Him. He is the One who did not and does not will to be the One He is—the eternal Son—without also being the Son of Man.[80]

This is not a line of thought that Barth ever modifies in the *Church Dogmatics*, nor does he present another position over against or alongside it. More than a nod toward Alexandria, Barth is endorsing its most basic concern. To be sure, he has also done justice to the Antiochene emphasis that Jesus Christ is indeed *vere homo* and as such is not to be confused with God. Yet with respect to the basic disagreement that distinguishes Alexandrian and Antiochene Christologies—the question of whether the acting subject of the incarnation is the Son of God or both the Son of God and the man Jesus—Barth sides squarely and unswervingly with the Alexandrian concern. That having been said, Barth's covenantal-actualistic construal of the hypostatic union, and his insistence that Jesus Christ is the Subject of election (and therefore eternally *to be* incarnate), obviously constitute a massive correction of the entire drift of classical Christology, whether Antiochene, Alexandrian, or otherwise. While Barth takes these ancient debates with utter seriousness, his position cannot be classified neatly as Alexandrian or Antiochene. Barth's Christology bursts through these categories, while incorporating insights from each.

It should be clear by now why the specification of the exact character of the human side of the hypostatic union is of such decisive significance. Because Jesus Christ is a human as the Son of God, his humanity "has a direct relevance for all other men, and in all the uniqueness in which it is an event in Jesus Christ His incarnation signifies the promise of the basic alteration and determination of what we all are as men. In Jesus Christ it is not merely one man, but the *humanum* of all men, which is posited and exalted as such to unity with God."[81] If the content of his exaltation is elevation to the freedom of obedience, and if this is the determination that human essence receives objectively in him, then humanity is concretely realized in obedience corresponding to his obedience.[82]

"THE HOLY ONE AND THE SAINTS" (*CD* § 66.2)

Barth's treatment of sanctification in paragraph sixty-six includes a section titled "The Holy One and the Saints." This section contributes nothing that would count as a significant development of Barth's understanding of participation in Christ. This claim will likely come as a surprise to many who have read this section, since it is here that Barth, following Calvin, treats sanctification as *participatio Christi*. But as I have tried to show throughout this study, virtually the whole of the *Church Dogmatics* is set forth within the framework of objective and subjective participation in Christ. Thus, when in the opening paragraph of "The Holy One and the Saints" we read the following lead sentence, we find that we are in familiar territory:

> The sanctification of man, his conversion to God, is, like his justification, a transformation, a new determination, which has taken place *de jure* for the world and therefore for all men. *De facto*, however, it is not known by all men, just as justification has not *de facto* been grasped and acknowledged and known and confessed by all men, but only by those who are awakened to faith. It is the people of these men which has also known sanctification. . . . What has come to it *de facto* has come to all men *de jure*.[83]

Throughout this section, Barth reiterates a number of his most characteristic concerns. Yet he adds nothing essential to his overall teaching concerning participation in Christ, and therefore I have chosen to omit treatment of this section entirely. I pause to mention this only because most people familiar with *CD* IV/2 would expect this section to be treated extensively in a study examining Barth's understanding of participation in Christ. Yet the fact remains that it contributes nothing uniquely important to the topic.

"THE GOAL OF VOCATION" (*CD* § 71.3)

We will now turn our attention to *CD* IV/3. In paragraph fifty-eight of *CD* IV/1 Barth makes the penetrating observation that seventeenth-century Protestant Orthodoxy's inability to adequately relate the prophetic to the priestly and kingly offices led directly to the "fatal" move of the Enlightenment, i.e., the absolutization of the prophetic office and the near-total dismissal of the other two offices.[84] "That this may not happen again," in *CD* IV/3 Barth offers a full-scale treatment of the *munus propheticum*, in which he argues that the reconciliation accomplished in Jesus Christ "shines out and avails and is effective in Him."[85] Jesus Christ guarantees that the truth of his existence, the fulfillment of reconciliation in him, will be heard and received and embraced by those for whom it was accomplished, and he does so by "attesting Himself," by being his own "authentic witness."[86] The whole of Barth's treatment of the prophetic office in *CD* IV/3 is an elaboration of the summary statement that "Jesus Christ is the actuality of the atonement, and as such the truth of it which speaks for itself."[87] Jesus Christ discloses himself in the glory of his victorious work as Mediator between God and humanity. He is the prophet of the reconciliation that he accomplishes: "As He lives, Jesus Christ speaks for Himself."[88] He does not leave it to someone or something else to correlate what he has accomplished with those for whom he has accomplished it. Instead:

> In His glory He radiates His being and action for the world out from Himself into the world in order that it may share it. In His revelation, shining as light, He discloses and manifests and announces and imparts Himself, moving out from Himself to where He and His being and work are not yet known and perceived.[89]

Jesus Christ, risen from the dead, victorious over the powers and principalities, manifests himself in the power of the Holy Spirit, glorifies himself, makes himself known, reveals himself as the reconciler of the world, and creates a confessing community that witnesses to him as Lord. Those are the basic contents of Barth's extraordinarily rich treatment of the *munus propheticum*.[90]

The section within *CD* IV/3 that I will examine is titled "The Goal of Vocation."[91] When, in the power of the Holy Spirit, the resurrected Jesus Christ addresses a person and she becomes a hearer of the Word, she is "illuminated, awakened and set in motion."[92] The end to which she is set in motion, the telos of vocation, Barth argues in this section, is union with Christ. Throughout this study, I have argued that Barth's understanding of participation in Christ is thoroughly actualistic in character. His description of union with Christ in this section crowns his previous teaching concerning participation in Christ and seals the argument that I have been making in this study.

Life in Analogy to Jesus Christ

In its simplest form, the purpose of vocation is that one "should become a Christian, a *homo christianus*."[93] Jesus Christ creates Christians as he calls them, and he calls them simply—yet wholly and exclusively—to be attached to him. "In the well-known and clear-cut phrase of Luther, 'I believe that Jesus Christ is my Lord.' This includes and expresses everything that he is and does specifically for the Christian and the whole relationship of the Christian to Him."[94] Vocation establishes a personal relationship which is characterized on the human side by pure freedom in obedience. Christian existence "is not an angelic, let alone a divine form."[95] It is human life determined and shaped by the Word of God, an existence analogous to Jesus Christ's life as the Son of God.

> [T]he distinctive feature of the being of Christians as the children of God thus consists decisively and dominatingly in the fact that, as those whom

Jesus Christ has called and calls to Himself in the work of His Spirit, they exist in particular proximity to Him and therefore in analogy to what He is. . . . He is originally the Son of God. And in analogy and correspondence, which means with real similarity, for all the dissimilarity, they may become sons of God. Their new and distinctive being as Christians is their being in this real similarity, for all the dissimilarity, to His being as the Son of God.[96]

Thus, the being of the children of God "does not have to become active," because it is a being *in* action.[97] This action is the human Yes to God, which corresponds to God's Yes to humanity in Jesus Christ. As Barth writes, "All are elected and ordained for fellowship with Jesus Christ. All move towards it. It is waiting for all. But it is one thing to be elected for it and another thing to be set in it. The latter is the distinctive thing which takes place in the calling of man and makes him a Christian."[98] Christian existence is grounded in election and occurs as its active realization. It is life in analogy to Jesus Christ's life. Thus, to clarify a point that has been just beneath the surface throughout this study, Barth is affirming an analogy of being between God and human creatures. He is emphatic that the analogy does not belong to created nature as such and never exists apart from the immediate action of God's sovereign grace. But he also affirms that in the obedience of active participation in Christ, in the event of the union and communion of divine-human fellowship, human being is analogous to the being of Jesus Christ (whose life history is altogether one of divine-human obedience), and therefore human being is analogous to the being of God.

The Event of *Koinōnia*

Having reached this point, Barth is now ready to tell us that the relationship he has been describing is a fellowship (*koinōnia*) with Jesus Christ (1 Cor. 1:9). After introducing this term, he offers a formal definition of its meaning:

> In the language of the New Testament, κοινωνία or *communicatio* is a relationship between two persons in which these are brought into perfect mutual co-ordination within the framework of a definite order, yet with no destruction of their two-sided identity and particularity, but rather in its confirmation and expression. We have such a relationship, such fellowship and therefore mutual coordination [*gegenseitige Zuordnung*], in unique perfection in the relationship of man to Jesus Christ in which he is set when his vocation takes place.[99]

Thus, the fellowship established in the event of vocation is a relationship with three aspects:

1. It is definitely ordered (i.e., it is a relationship of lordship and service).

2. Jesus Christ and the individual enjoy "perfect mutual coordination" one with the other.

3. Jesus Christ and the individual each retain their particularity and distinction from one another.

Barth highlights the event-character of *koinōnia* by immediately offering a synonym for this fellowship: discipleship. "The simplest description of this fellowship, which reveals at once its distinctive order and perfection, is that which is preferred in the Gospels, namely, that he is called to the discipleship of Jesus Christ."[100] Jesus Christ leads and the disciple obeys. That is the irreversible order of their relationship. Fellowship with Jesus Christ "will always be a venture in which no man can wait for or rely on others, as though they could represent him or make the leap for him. Even in the community and therefore with other Christians, he can believe, obey and confess only in his own person and on his own responsibility."[101]

Moreover, the sovereignty of Jesus Christ's action creates the intimacy of *koinōnia* by liberating the individual to be who she is in him. Jesus Christ does not exercise his sovereignty by brute and overwhelming force. He does not coerce his disciples into obedience. Rather, he opens them up from the inside, so to speak.

> For the gift and work of the Holy Spirit as the divine power of His Word is that, while Jesus Christ encounters man in it with alien majesty, He does not remain thus, nor is He merely a strange, superior Lord disposing concerning him in majesty from without. On the contrary, even as such, without ceasing to be the Lord or forfeiting His transcendence, but rather in its exercise, He gives and imparts Himself to him, entering into him as his Lord in all His majesty and setting up His throne within him. Thus His control, as that of the owner over his possession, becomes the most truly distinctive feature of this man, the center and basis of his human existence, the axiom of his freest thinking and utterance, the origin of his freest volition and action, in short the principle of his spontaneous being [*Prinzip seines spontanen Daseins*]. The gift and work of the Holy Spirit as the divine power of the Word of vocation is the placing of man in this fellowship with Him, namely, with the being, will and action of Jesus Christ.[102]

Thus as Jesus Christ encounters those whom he calls, he illuminates and awakens them to their true being—a being in the freedom of his service. In so doing he becomes the ruling principle of their lives, and as such he awakens them to the freedom and spontaneity of their own truest selves.[103] It is precisely in ruling them in this way that Jesus Christ enters Christians and becomes one with them.

Union with Christ

Having reached this point, Barth proceeds once again to clarify the content of this relationship by designating it with another term: union with Christ. For the purposes of this study, it is important to notice that Barth places his description of union with Christ at just this point. By embedding his treatment of union with Christ within a thoroughly actualistic description of the meaning of divine-human fellowship, and by describing the meaning and content of union with Christ entirely within that framework, it becomes clear that union with Christ as Barth describes it here is a synonym for the de facto participation in Christ that I have been describing throughout this study. Just as the telos of objective participation in Christ is active participation, so too the telos of vocation is union with Christ. In this event, as Barth puts it in this section, the believer "delivers himself *de facto* to the One to whom he belongs *de iure*."[104]

Barth contrasts what he means by union with Christ with the concept of mysticism. If the New Testament understanding of union with Christ could possibly be described as mysticism, "it would have to be a mysticism *sui generis* in this context. There can certainly be no question of what is usually denoted by the term in this relationship."[105] Barth lists four ways in which union with Christ differs from mysticism:

1. Union with Christ is not an experience "induced by a psychical and intellectual concentration, deepening and elevating of the human self-consciousness."[106] Barth eschews such an idea, viewing it as a Pelagian denial of God's grace. Yet he does not deny that union with Christ involves experience. How could it not involve experience when it is a real and total union? The Christian is united with Jesus Christ in the whole of his existence, and therefore in the whole of his experience. Barth's point is rather that "neither his receiving nor his acting in this fellowship is the product or work of his own skill."[107]

2. Union with Christ will never involve the elimination of "the true confrontation of God and man" because if this confrontation were eliminated, the union could not be an event of discipleship.[108]

3. Union with Christ is personal, not impersonal. It does not reduce the believer to silence. God's call finds its proper response in the praise of joyful obedience, not silence. It calls forth adoration, not apophasis.

4. Union with Christ does not overcome the "distinction between the Creator and creature or the antithesis between the Holy One and sinners, nor any establishment of the kind of equilibrium which may exist between things but can never obtain between persons, and especially between the divine Jesus Christ and human persons."[109] Union with Christ is a "fellowship of encounter" (*Gemeinschaft in der Begegnung*) between the grace of God and sinful human beings, and thus always

"includes a judgment passed on man."[110] For this reason, even in the midst of this union, the grace of Jesus Christ "does not cease to demand that individuals keep their distance."[111] Rather than being a diminution of the dignity of the person addressed by the Word, this distance guarantees the freedom of the Christian within the union because without this space the creature could only be overwhelmed by God's action. The believer is free precisely because within the intimacy of this union, God gives her space to live and act and have her being.

After making these clarifications, Barth concludes (against Albert Schweitzer and others, although he mentions no writers by name) that the term "Christ-mysticism" could only properly be used within a framework that expressly states these limits. And since there is "no compelling reason" to insist on using the term, Barth recommends avoiding it and thus the confusion it might create.[112]

Having clarified that union with Christ is a union in *distinction*, he moves on to emphasize that it is a *union* in distinction, and once again he stresses that it is a union in *action*. Union with Christ is a "true, total and indissoluble union" precisely because Christ and Christians have their "own independence, uniqueness and activity."[113] In the coming together of the totally self-giving action of the Lord and the correspondingly total response of his servants, "this self-giving Christ and the Christian become and are a single totality, a fluid and differentiated but genuine and solid unity."[114] As Jesus Christ calls Christians, he makes them alive by making them his witnesses. In doing so, he enters them and unites himself to them. Notice that Barth is not saying that Jesus Christ first makes people alive and then makes them his witnesses, but rather that he makes them alive *by* making them his witnesses. Union with Christ is not merely the privatistic reception of gifts. It is rather the perfect mutual coordination of Jesus Christ's active calling and the correspondingly active human response of witness to the grace and greatness of God.

> In this perfect fellowship the one Christ as the only original Son of God, beside whom there can be no other, is always the One who gives, commands and precedes, and the other, the *homo christianus*, whom He makes His brother and therefore a child of God, is always the one who receives, obeys and follows. The former is the Word of God in person; the latter, like John the Baptist in the Fourth Gospel, is His witness. In this distinction, of course neither remains alone. Both become a totality. For it is not too great or small a thing for Christ to give Himself to the Christian, to cause His own life to be that of the Christian, to make Himself his with all that this necessarily implies. This is the high reality of His vocation to the extent that this takes place and is to be understood as His union with the Christian.[115]

Union with Christ is the event of this "differentiated fellowship of action."[116]

This is a fitting point at which to end this study. For it demonstrates once and for all that Barth's comment concerning his treatment of the hypostatic union—that "thinking and speaking in pure concepts of movement, we have re-translated that whole phenomenology into the sphere of a history"[117]—applies also, and for just that reason, to his understanding of participation in Christ. Jesus Christ's whole life history is one of obedience—divine obedience (*göttlichen Gehorsam*) and corresponding human obedience.[118] Both movements are grounded in the eternal decision of election in which the Son freely chooses to offer himself in obedience to the Father's decision to offer him up. In the temporal occurrence of this eternal decision, both divine and human being are enacted and realized in obedience, albeit in different ways. The free obedience of the Son of God is the antecedent self-giving of God to the creature. The corresponding free obedience of the Son of Man is the subsequent active reception of this gift. Jesus Christ is the perfect fellowship of this divine giving and human receiving. As such, he establishes the truth of human being, and he summons those for whom this truth has been established to embrace it by joining themselves to him. This summons takes the form of God's good, sovereign, and definite command. As this command is heard and obeyed, humanity is realized. And in the fellowship of this encounter, "we are united to Jesus Christ and in Jesus Christ to God Himself."[119]

CONCLUSION

Having set forth Barth's teaching concerning participation in Christ in the previous chapters, I would like to conclude with a brief examination of two aspects of his thought that call for further attention: his rejection of the sacraments and his affirmation of the *simul peccator et sanctus* teaching. I will then draw out some of the ecumenical significance of Barth's view by comparing it with Orthodox understandings of *theosis*. Thus, rather than using this space to summarize the work as a whole, I have chosen instead to address two problematic areas of Barth's view and then to show how the results of the study enable us to rethink Barth's relationship to a major stream of the church's reflection on the meaning of salvation.

BAPTISM AND THE LORD'S SUPPER

Since there is certainly an ecclesial dimension to Barth's understanding of participation in Christ, one will perhaps wonder why I have chosen not to offer a full treatment of Barth's ecclesiology. The answer is quite simple. While elucidating Barth's ecclesiology would have constituted a filling out of the interpretation already set forth here, it would not have meant a significant material contribution to it.[1] Barth's ecclesiology derives from doctrines that are more basic to his thought, doctrines that I have dealt with in detail, such as election and Christology.[2] Nevertheless, many readers, especially those less familiar with Barth's thought, will rightly wonder why baptism and the Lord's Supper do not figure more centrally (or at all) in Barth's understanding of participation in Christ. In light of passages such as Romans 6:3–5 and Galatians 3:27–28, on the one hand, and 1 Corinthians 10:16–18, on the other, how could they not? Barth did not live to complete his treatment of the Lord's Supper in the *Church Dogmatics*, but his teaching on baptism is sufficient to answer the question.

In addition to his exegetical and sociological arguments against sacramental views of baptism, the answer to the question has everything to do with Barth's understanding of the relationship between de jure and de facto participation in Christ. Barth divided the baptism fragment into two sections: "Baptism with the Spirit" and "Baptism with Water."[3] The latter, which includes his rejection of infant baptism, is the more well known, but the key dogmatic decisions are made in the first section. And as it turns out, "Baptism with the Spirit" is a reflection on the nature of the transition from de jure to de facto participation in Christ—a reflection, moreover, that is entirely consistent with his earlier teaching on the matter.

Discipleship is a transition from death to life, an event altogether grounded in the objective conversion of humanity to God in Jesus Christ. Jesus Christ's history "reaches beyond itself"[4] in such a way that the Christian is now a person to "whom Jesus Christ has given not just a potential, but an actual share in that history."[5] Thus, Jesus Christ's history "is not sterile. It is a fruitful history which newly shapes every human life. Having taken place *extra nos*, it also works *in nobis*, introducing a new being of every man."[6] According to Barth:

> The whole point is that here, as everywhere, the omnicausality of God must not be construed as His sole causality. The divine change in whose accomplishment a man becomes a Christian is an event of true intercourse between God and man. If it undoubtedly has its origin in God's initiative, no less indisputably man is not ignored or passed over in it. He is taken seriously as an independent creature of God. He is not run down and overpowered, but set on his own feet. . . . The history of Jesus Christ, then, does not destroy a man's own history. In virtue of it this history becomes a new history, but it is still his own history.[7]

On the basis of these observations, Barth rejects both "christomonism" and "anthropomonism," the former because it denies the reality of the de facto, the latter because it denies the reality of the de jure.[8] In other words, "christomonism" erases the Christian, while "anthropomonism" erases Christ. But "a true Christocentricity," Barth claims, will avoid both errors.[9] But how will it do so? How does the transition from de jure to de facto happen?

Barth's answer to this question provides the rationale for his rejection of infant baptism in the subsequent section. The transition takes place, he argues, as Jesus Christ, raised from the dead and present in the power of his perfect history, proclaims "in every age and place" that his history is the history of the salvation of the world.[10] When he is heard and received, when human beings are renewed and awakened to their new life in him, when they respond in obedient gratitude to his grace, this takes place as the work of the Holy Spirit.[11] The telos of de jure participation in Christ is de facto participation in Christ, and the Holy Spirit is the teleological power of this transition. Thus, the work of the Spirit:

is not a different work, a second work alongside, behind and after the work of the reconciling covenant action of the one God accomplished in the history of Jesus Christ and manifested in his resurrection. It is the one divine work in its movement, its concrete reference, to specific men, wherein for the first time it reaches its goal. The work of the Holy Spirit is concerned with the Word which manifests this history in its access and entry into the hearts and consciences of specific men.[12]

Barth is obviously holding the work of the Spirit and the work of Christ in the closest possible connection.[13] The resurrection of Jesus Christ from the dead and the work of the Holy Spirit "are the two factors, or, as one may and should finally say, the two forms of the one factor" in which human beings are converted from death to life, from enmity toward God to faith in him.[14] Barth calls this conversion, this "divine change in a man's life," this response of human faithfulness to God's faithfulness, "baptism with the Holy Spirit."[15]

Baptism with the Spirit is effective, causative, even creative action on man and in man. It is, indeed, divinely effective, divinely causative, divinely creative. . . . It cleanses, renews and changes man truly and totally. . . . All this is to be taken realistically, not just significantly and figuratively.[16]

Thus, in response to the original question, Barth accounts for the transition from de jure to de facto participation in Christ, not with a sacramental doctrine of baptism, but with a Christocentric pneumatology and a theology of the resurrection of Jesus Christ. According to Barth, "the beginning of the Christian life takes place in a direct self-attestation and self-impartation of the living Jesus Christ."[17] Jesus Christ baptizes with the Holy Spirit, affecting the transition from de jure to de facto participation in Christ, and he "does not delegate this work to other factors, not even to His community."[18] Therefore, "the Church is neither author, dispenser, nor mediator of grace and its revelation."[19] Water baptism is a human act of obedience, grounded in Spirit baptism and attesting it, but nevertheless distinct from Spirit baptism, just as gratitude is grounded in and attests grace while remaining distinct from it. Therefore, baptism and the Lord's Supper are not divinely appointed means of grace; they do not represent or mediate salvation, and therefore they are not sacraments.

Thus, Barth's position blocks any view, no matter how attentive to the proper distinction and ordering between divine and human action, that might impinge upon God's freedom and sovereignty in the bestowal of grace and salvation. Not only does it cohere with the fundamental impulses of his theology as a whole,[20] it also offers a stark alternative to

Roman Catholic and liberal Protestant accounts of the way that grace becomes subjectively effective within the lives of believers.[21] Yet after discerning the motivating reasons behind Barth's rejection of the sacraments, and appreciating his many penetrating observations, one still wonders whether the dangers that Barth saw lurking in sacramental views of baptism and the Lord's Supper (even versions within the Reformed tradition that he could affirm, however carefully, well into the 1940s) are *necessarily* as deleterious as he believed. And even if they are, it remains an open question whether or not a sacramental view of baptism and the Lord's Supper could be developed from within a Barthian perspective, i.e., in a way that would not trespass upon the freedom and sovereignty of God or the perfection of Jesus Christ's person and work, and indeed that would cohere with his pneumatology, theology of the resurrection, and indeed his view of participation in Christ in general.[22] Moreover, and especially importantly, one wonders whether Barth's position is as exegetically persuasive as he thought it was, i.e., whether it does adequate justice to all of the relevant New Testament texts, especially those which so closely link participation in Christ with baptism and the Lord's Supper. Barth's view certainly emerges consistently from patterns of thought that lie at the very center of his theology, indeed, patterns which I have highlighted throughout this study, but that, of course, is not reason enough to be persuaded by it, nor is it self-evident that those commitments *required* Barth to adopt the position that he did.

SIMUL PECCATOR ET SANCTUS?

Throughout this study I have highlighted Barth's commitment to the affirmation that Jesus Christ is himself grace, and therefore that we receive Christ's benefits only to the extent that we are joined to him. Grace never becomes our possession, since Jesus Christ never becomes our possession. However one might judge Barth's rejection of the *habitus* concept, it clearly stems from this basic insight. So too does his use of the *simul iustus et peccator* teaching, which Barth extends into the area of sanctification. It is the latter innovation that I would like to briefly examine.

The *simul iustus et peccator* doctrine affirms that in ourselves we remain totally sinful even as in Christ we are totally righteous. For Barth, this teaching guarantees that Jesus Christ will never be displaced from his place of supreme importance, since believers remain dependent on him at every moment. With this in mind, Barth's teaching concerning sanctification also becomes intelligible: our sanctification consists in participation in Jesus Christ's sanctification, and thus our sanctification, like our justification, is conceived as *aliena sanctitate; sanctitate Jesu Christi*. "Luther's *simul* (*totus*) *iustus, simul* (*totus*) *peccator* has thus to be applied strictly to sanctification."[23] This led Barth to coin a new term—*simul peccator et sanctus.*[24] Such a person, Barth writes, is:

> both the old man of yesterday and the new man of tomorrow. . . . is still the old and yet already the new, in complete and utter antithesis. . . . [T]he *vita christiana* in conversion is the event, the act, the history, in which at one and the same time man is still wholly the old man and already wholly the new—so powerful is the sin by which he is determined from behind, and so powerful the grace by which he is determined from before. . . . [T]here is an order and sequence in this *simul.* . . . The old and the new man are simultaneously present in the relationship of a *terminus a quo* and a *terminus ad quem.*[25]

Homo peccator has been displaced, has passed away, and yet somehow still persists in the present. *Homo sanctus* has been established as the future of humanity, which in obedience becomes present. Thus it is clear that for Barth, as for Luther before him, the *simul* doctrine denotes an eschatology.

Barth's emphasis on the totality of these two simultaneous determinations led him to draw the radical conclusion that de facto sanctification "takes place here below where there is no action that does not have the marks of sloth or can be anything but displeasing to God. This is true even of their lifting up of themselves, even of their looking to the Lord, which is their actions as saints."[26] This is an extreme and unnecessary assertion, one that ultimately cuts against Barth's affirmation of de facto participation in Christ.

Throughout this study, I have shown how Barth repeatedly stresses that de jure participation in Christ grounds, elicits, and guarantees de facto participation in Christ. In obedience, human beings are joined to Jesus Christ and are therefore holy. This fact should have led Barth to conclude that as this event takes place, there is nothing left to say about such people than that they are holy. They are, so to speak, wholly holy because they *are* in this act of theirs, and in this act of theirs they are joined to Jesus Christ. The question is, Does obedient human action correspond to God's gracious action or not? If it does, then there is no reason to say that it does not, which is what Barth seems to affirm when he says that even our good actions can only be displeasing to God and therefore require his justification.[27] Why would they require justification if they really are good actions—actions that correspond to God's action?

Barth's primary reason for drawing this conclusion seems to be that good human action does not arise from a person's "own heart or emotions or understanding or conscience, but has its origin in the power of the direction which has come to"[28] her in Jesus Christ. Barth insists that obedience takes place not by one's "own caprice, but by the will and touch and address and creation and gift of this Lord."[29] That is, of course, true. But because it is true, because God's grace actually elicits genuine human obedience, those acts of obedience are actually good. To have said so would not have jeopardized any of Barth's basic concerns, such as that Jesus Christ is himself grace; that grace is not a transferred condition; that human beings are holy and righteous only by virtue of their participation in Jesus Christ's holiness and righteousness; that holiness is categorical rather than partial; that good human action does not synergistically cooperate with divine action, but is ever dependent on it; that sin is an ever-present threat which, when embraced, constitutes a contradiction of true humanity, etc. Among other things, Barth's otherwise successful counter to the Roman Catholic charge that justification is a legal fiction is undermined to the extent that he casts doubt on the reality of the transformation of the believer that takes place in de facto participation. For these and numerous other reasons, Barth should simply have said that where and when obedience takes place by the power of the Holy Spirit, it is exclusively obedience, and therefore good human action. He does, of course, say this in places. But he denies it in other places, which was a mistake, and an unnecessary one at that.

While one could pursue any number of other critical questions about Barth's position, rather than doing so I would like to capitalize on the results of this study by exploring an area in which Barth's thought seems especially relevant to the ecumenical scene. I have argued throughout this study that for Barth participation in Christ is participation in God, and that while his theology appears altogether inimical to deification, on closer inspection it turns out not to be. In the following section, I will expand those arguments by showing some of the interesting and significant ways that Barth's view converges with Orthodox descriptions of *theosis*. My aim is to show that in addition to constituting a formidable challenge to traditional ways of construing *theosis*, Barth also offers a sympathetic and important contribution to that tradition of thought.

BARTH AND ORTHODOXY ON *THEOSIS*

Theosis is ubiquitous within contemporary theology. For Orthodoxy, humanity's eschatological goal, realized progressively within the life of believers in time, is participation in the triune being of God. As God freely shares his life with believers, believers are freely assimilated to that life and thereby deified, i.e., by grace they become "gods" (*theoi*).[30] This teaching, "the central dogma of Orthodoxy,"[31] and inseparably related to every dogmatic locus, is gaining ever-increasing attention outside of Orthodoxy. While Orthodoxy is not a monolithic entity, and *theosis* is not a doctrine affirmed by the Orthodox alone, nevertheless the teaching has long been associated with Orthodoxy, and the rediscovery of this teaching by non-Orthodox Christians can largely be traced back to engagement, in one way or another, with Orthodoxy. *Theosis* has figured significantly, and often centrally, in ecumenical dialogues between Orthodox and Lutherans[32]; Reformed and Orthodox[33]; Orthodox and Anglicans[34]; and, especially prominent recently, between Lutherans and Catholics.[35] Apart from these official dialogues, *theosis* has been sympathetically treated by scholars from within most major branches of Christianity.[36] The cumulative result of scholarly engagement with this issue is an emerging consensus that the *Christian* understanding of salvation, whatever else it may involve and however it may be construed, somehow includes participation in God's being. This truth, which the Orthodox understanding of *theosis* explicates, is not simply a teaching of Orthodoxy, but of the church catholic.[37]

Yet for just this reason, one would expect there to be considerable diversity in the meaning and development of this teaching across the various traditions. Consider the following statement: God became human to share his life with humans. While, for example, Vladimir Lossky and John Calvin might both have happily agreed with this formulation, one can easily imagine how quickly their respective explications of its meaning would diverge. And as one examines the history of Christian theology, one notices a wide variety of opinion regarding the meaning of human participation in the being of God. This is so not only across traditions, but within the patristic era itself. The best studies on *theosis* recognize this fact. For example, toward the end of her survey of *theosis* in the patristic period, which precedes her treatment of Thomas Aquinas and Gregory Palamas, A.N. Williams speaks of "considerable diversity in the ways various theologians describe deification."[38] Basil Studer writes that "research on divinization has been made very complex by the historical data themselves. Thus the relevant vocabulary has undergone a considerable evolution.... Moreover, the anthropological premises varied according to author.... The theological and Christological premises were equally diverse."[39] And Jules Gross, upon reaching the end of his study, finds it necessary to raise the following question: "But what exactly do they mean by deification? Is it a question of an exaggeration, as bold as it is devoid of meaning, or does the expression include a reality? Actually, none of the Greeks who employ the term *theosis* or its equivalents give a definition of it. But this vagueness itself allows them to accommodate, under the terminology to which they have recourse, a host of things which are neither on the same level nor of the same nature."[40]

Gross's observation is significant. The patristic and Orthodox resistance to overprecision in the description of deification gives the doctrine room to breathe and in so doing makes it all the more vital and appealing. The trade-offs, of course, are obvious. But who would disagree with Gross's observation concerning the church fathers that "their concrete and colorful manner of conceiving of and describing this mysterious reality has a great advantage since it enables us to grasp its richness more easily and live in it more directly"?[41] Recognition of this fact is not intended as a denial of a common core of concerns within all presentations of *theosis*. Far from it. Yet deification defies definition. It is a framework at once lively, diffuse, and fluid, capable of accommodating a variety of metaphors and insights. And as one recognizes this, an interesting question arises. As the theme of *theosis* continues to advance toward the forefront of contemporary theology, what is the significance for the present discussion of the fact that the concept itself admits of an astonishingly wide range of expositions?

However one might answer this question, at the very least it seems indisputable that the variegation of the theme presents an opportunity for fruitful contemporary inquiry. The roominess of the concept invites Christians from outside of Orthodoxy to learn from Orthodox teaching and also to explore the extent to which modes of thought within their own traditions significantly overlap Orthodox thought. Moreover, as various Christian communities continue the process of determining for themselves what it means to say that salvation involves human participation in the being of God, and as they test the systematic implications of this affirmation across the spectrum of Christian doctrine, they do so in interaction with a doctrine that would benefit from further clarification. Specifically, the various aspects of the ontology of the event require greater elucidation. Human beings, by grace, participate in God's being. What are the conditions for the possibility of this occurrence? What specifically happens in this event? How does it happen? What is the mode of its occurrence? What is the proper way to conceptualize the nature of the *distinction* between God and human beings *within* this union? These are a few of the many questions that require clarification within the present discussion.

Throughout this study I have shown that Barth's understanding of participation in Christ provides specific and illuminating answers to these and many other related and significant questions. Moreover his teaching concerning participation in Christ should be understood as a constructive contribution to the church's tradition of reflection on the meaning of human participation in the being of God and not merely a rejection of that tradition. To be sure, Barth offers a specifically Reformed way of thinking through these issues, and as such he is careful to respect the distinction between the Creator and his creatures. But he writes for the whole church, not merely a part of it, and he does so as a contributor to a discussion that has been taking place within the church through the centuries. Barth learns from this discussion, criticizes it, and attempts to redirect it, but he never dismisses it. He broadly acknowledges the concerns of the proponents of *theosis* in its various forms, even if he differs significantly in how he thinks those concerns should best be met. Barth's aim is not to demolish this tradition of thought, but to reconstruct it. His understanding of participation in Christ is a sympathetic and innovative attempt to contribute to the conversation by offering a covenantal-historical construal of what it means for human beings to participate in God. If Barth is a critic of all existing models of deification, he is so as an insider to the discussion, as someone who agrees with the validity and importance of the questions, and who intends to think the issue through from its dynamic center in Jesus Christ. Thus it is entirely consonant with Barth's theology as a whole, to find him arguing at the start of his doctrine of reconciliation that salvation "consists in participation in the being of God" (*in der Teilnahme am Sein Gottes besteht*) and indeed that "the coming of this salvation is the grace of God—using the word in its narrower and most proper sense."[42]

This way of stating Barth's relationship to the history of the church's reflection on deification will puzzle many readers. If ever there was an enemy of deification, was it not Barth? How can Barth be a contributor to the church's clarification of the meaning of human participation in the triune being of God when he rejects deification literally hundreds of times throughout the *Church Dogmatics*? Consider just a few of the ways that Barth and Orthodoxy differ significantly on the matter of participation in the being of God:[43]

1. If human beings participate in God's being, God's being must, in some way, be participable. Barth does not affirm the distinction, widely (although not universally) held within Orthodoxy, between divine essence and energies, and he defends the *filioque*. Therefore their respective doctrines of God yield differing understandings of the meaning of human participation in God's being.

2. Participation in God's life is a reality for human beings because it is a reality in Jesus Christ. Barth and Orthodoxy agree on this point. Yet their Christologies differ significantly—especially regarding the *communicatio idiomatum*—and therefore so too do their descriptions of the meaning of participation in God's life. Unlike the Orthodox, Barth does not think that Jesus' human nature is deified (in the sense of receiving and possessing divine "qualities" or "attributes"), and therefore he denies that human participation in the being of God involves such a transfer.

3. The Orthodox synergistic construal of the relationship between divine and human action is at odds with Barth's understanding of that relationship. Both agree that human participation in God occurs in human freedom, but their conceptions of the meaning of participation will differ along with their differing views of human freedom, the *imago Dei*, and sin.

4. Whereas the doctrine of election is centrally significant for Barth's understanding of human participation in God's life and touches every

aspect of it, that doctrine plays virtually no role in Orthodox descriptions of *theosis*. Neither does Orthodoxy emphasize the covenant in the way that Barth does.

5. The sacraments (mysteries) often figure centrally in Orthodox discussions of *theosis*, but, as we have seen, that is not the case with Barth's understanding of human participation in God. In addition to his repudiation of sacramental mediation in general, Barth's actualistic ontology is incompatible with the common affirmation that grace is infused into the soul of the believer through the sacraments.[44]

There are, of course, other and important differences between Barth's conception of the meaning of human participation in God and that of the Orthodox. I do not deny that such differences exist nor do I want to argue for some kind of rapprochement by smoothing them out. I am arguing, rather, that Barth is a contributor to the church's history of reflection on this important issue, and that the quality of his contribution merits consideration within the present discussion. The following are just a few of the areas where their concerns overlap considerably:

1. Both Barth and Orthodoxy conceive of participation in God teleologically and eschatologically. Participation in God represents the "ultimate destiny" of humanity.[45] For Barth, this means the fulfillment of a perfect reality (i.e., the objective participation of all humanity in Christ is fulfilled as believers subjectively participate in Christ), whereas for the Orthodox the teleological movement is conceived along more gradual lines, as the final realization of a partial beginning.[46] Nevertheless, both agree that participation in God is a teleological and eschatological concept.

2. Both Barth and Orthodoxy insist that participation in God is not the abolition of true humanity, but its realization. Each works this out in a different way, but both agree that participation in God "does not suppress humanity, but makes humanity truly human."[47] Moreover, they agree that while the union between God and human beings is real, it is real as a union in distinction.[48]

3. For much of Orthodoxy, God's nature (*ousia*) is unapproachable, unknowable, and impartible. Deification is participation in God's energies. Nevertheless, "these energies are not something that exists apart from God, not a gift which God confers upon humans; they are God Himself in His action and revelation to the world. God exists complete and entire in each of His divine energies."[49] Barth does not share this distinction between essence and energies, but he affirms something analogous to it. According to Barth, that which most basically distinguishes God from all else is his gracious and sovereign *action*. This action is God's alone. God does not share it. God's being is in-act, and God's act is sovereign and gracious. But God freely shares *himself* with us. And he does

so by including us in this action of his and therefore in himself. In the event of the union of God's free primary action and our correspondingly free secondary response, we are given a creaturely share in God's being. Thus, for both Barth and Orthodoxy, God's "nature" is imparticible even as human beings really participate in God.

4. Barth's actualistic anthropology, his insistence that human "being" does not precede human action, but rather is in-act, overlaps with what Meyendorff describes as "the central theme, or intuition, of Byzantine theology," which, he writes, "is that man's nature is not a static, 'closed,' autonomous entity, but a dynamic reality, determined in its very existence by its relationship to God," such that "his very nature is truly itself only as much as it exists 'in God' or 'in grace.'"[50] I have already noted the divergent ways in which Barth and Orthodoxy conceive of nature and grace, and it goes without saying that Barth's Christocentric framework for understanding created nature is very different from that of Orthodoxy. Nevertheless, there is an important shared emphasis among them that human nature is only properly described in dynamic, active, and one might even say kinetic terms. What Meyendorff writes of Orthodoxy could, in its own way, apply equally well to Barth: "The *logos* of every creature consists, therefore, in being essentially *active*; there is no 'nature' without 'energy' or movement."[51] Furthermore, both agree that participation in God is the event in which human nature is actively realized.

Many other areas of shared concern could be mentioned. Rather than pursuing them, however, I will conclude with one final observation. If a set of core criteria common to all expositions of *theosis* could be determined, and if it could be shown that Barth's theology offers a significant contribution to the church's thinking about these issues, then the claim that Barth is an insider and contributor to the church's history of reflection on the theme of participation in God would be strengthened even further.

In her summary of the patristic doctrine of *theosis*, Williams offers just such a list. After acknowledging "considerable diversity in the ways various theologians describe deification," she observes that nonetheless, "there is a firm core that distinguishes this doctrine from some other model of sanctification."[52] According to Williams, four criteria must be met: "Where we find the ideas of [a] participation in divine life, [b] union with God and [c] humanity portrayed as human destiny, and [d] a mode of articulating divine transcendence in this context, we can say we are dealing with a doctrine of deification."[53]

In this study, I have shown that Barth's understanding of participation in Christ meets all of these criteria—as well as others not mentioned here. It does so in a uniquely Christocentric, historical, and covenantal way, but it certainly does so. Barth shares many of the basic convictions upheld by those who affirm *theosis*, and he addresses many of the same dogmatic issues which that teaching presents. The distinctive genius of his position, and his fundamental contribution to the church's thinking on the matter, is the unswerving way that he attempts to think through every aspect of the meaning of participation in God from its dynamic center in the living history of Jesus Christ himself as attested by Holy Scripture. Sadly, the church has hardly begun to perceive Barth's achievement on this front. And it has been especially inattentive to the unique way that his Christology enables him to clearly and powerfully articulate a dogmatically integrated vision of human participation in God, which affirms the dynamic reality and intimacy of that union, and at the same time preserves the ineradicable distinction that remains between the Lord and his servants even within it. My aim throughout this study has been to elucidate the results of that process as it unfolds throughout the *Church Dogmatics*. The longer one reflects on this material, the more one realizes how deeply traditional and daringly innovative, deceptively simple and surprisingly counterintuitive Barth's view of participation in Christ is. If the basic argument of this study is accurate, then the question should not be whether Barth's theology provides valuable resources for the church's ongoing work of clarifying and articulating its message of salvation as participation in the being of God. That much, I hope, is now beyond dispute. Instead, the pressing question is whether the church will notice. Barth was fond of pointing out that church unity is not created but discovered. If his distinctive understanding of participation in God could somehow contribute to this ongoing discovery, and to the church's clarification of its witness in the world, that would be a valuable thing indeed.

NOTES

INTRODUCTION

1. "How does one really come to find the solution of all theological questions in Christ? . . . It happens when one resolutely and persistently seeks in Christ and is then able to make the discovery that in fact it is to be found in him: *in quo* sunt *omnes thesauri sapientiae et scientiae absconditi* (Colossians 2: 3)." (Quoted in Eberhard Busch, *Karl Barth: His Life from Letters and Autobiographical Texts*, trans. John Bowden [Philadelphia: Fortress Press, 1976], 380.)

2. Given the extraordinary importance of the theme of participation in Christ in Barth's theology, it is remarkable that so few studies have been devoted to it. The earliest treatment is a dissertation by Bradley Hanson ("Hope and Participation in Christ: A Study in the Theology of Barth and Pannenberg" [ThD diss., Princeton Theological Seminary, 1970]) in which Barth's teaching concerning participation is set forth and then compared (unfavorably) to that of Wolfhart Pannenberg. Three decades later, David Stubbs's problematic dissertation ("Sanctification as Participation in Christ: Working through the Pauline and Kantian Legacies in Karl Barth's Theology of Sanctification" [PhD diss., Duke University, 2001]) argues that participation in Christ is the central theme in Barth's doctrine of sanctification. These are the only two dissertation-length treatments of the subject. The only article-length treatment is by Daniel Migliore ("Participatio Christi: The Central Theme in Barth's Doctrine of Sanctification" in *Zeitschrift für dialektische Theologie* 18 [2002]: 286–307). For an in-depth presentation and critique of the first two studies, a shorter and positive treatment of Migliore's article, and an analysis of George Hunsinger's important treatment of the theme, see the first chapter of my dissertation ("A Differentiated Fellowship of Action: Participation in Christ in Karl Barth's *Church Dogmatics*" [PhD diss., Princeton Theological Seminary, 2005]).

3. Karl Barth, *Church Dogmatics* IV/2: *The Doctrine of Reconciliation*, ed. G. W. Bromiley and T. F. Torrance, trans. G. W. Bromiley (Edinburgh: T. & T. Clark, 1958), 511–33.

4. Barth, *Church Dogmatics* I/1: *The Doctrine of the Word of God*, 2d ed., ed. G. W. Bromiley and T. F. Torrance, trans. G. W. Bromiley (Edinburgh: T. & T. Clark, 1975), 240.

5. Barth, *CD* I/1:241; *KD* I/1:254.

6. *Pace* Kurt Anders Richardson's claim that the *Church Dogmatics* ought to be read from back to front, as well as his assertion that as the *Church Dogmatics* develops "there is a gradual letting go of an earlier emphasis on *participation* in God in

favor of gracious *correspondence* to God in human obedience" (Kurt Anders Richardson, *Reading Karl Barth: New Directions for North American Theology* [Grand Rapids: Baker Academic, 2004], 10). I will show that participation does not give way to correspondence as the *Church Dogmatics* unfolds and also that Barth's thought on these matters cannot be grasped if these two categories are set against one another.

7. Barth's best interpreters complain that his work is all too often caricatured by misinformed critics. For example, Eberhard Jüngel admits that he is "astonished" and "perplexed" by much of what passes for Barth scholarship (*Karl Barth: A Theological Legacy*, trans. Garrett Paul [Philadelphia: Westminster Press, 1986], 14) and George Hunsinger states that "reading what the critics have to say of Barth's theology is usually like looking at an old map, the kind drafted before the dawn of modern cartography in the eighteenth century. Certain basic aspects of the theology may be present, but the distortion factor is high" (George Hunsinger, *How to Read Karl Barth: The Shape of His Theology* [New York: Oxford University Press, 1991], x).

8. Barth, *Evangelical Theology: An Introduction*, trans. Grover Foley (Grand Rapids: Eerdmans, 1963), 165. Commenting on this passage, Eberhard Jüngel notes: "Barth diligently adhered to this insight. Diligence was the source of his genius. He was supremely a worker. He remained a man who was always beginning" (*Karl Barth: A Theological Legacy*, 19).

CHAPTER 1

1. Barth, *CD* I/1:136.

2. Ibid., 241. When quoting from the *Church Dogmatics*, I have chosen to retain Barth's conventional use of the masculine form to indicate gender-neutral pronouns because my attempts to uniformly revise the translations often resulted in sentences that were artificial and at times misleading. While admittedly not much of a counterbalance, the reader will notice that whereas Barth consistently used the masculine form to indicate epicene pronouns, I consistently use the feminine form.

3. Ibid.; *KD* I/1:254.

4. Karl Barth, *Die Christliche Dogmatik im Entwurf* (Zurich: TVZ, 1982).

5. Barth, *CD* I/1:126–27.

6. Ibid., 126.

7. Ibid., 127. For more on Barth's doctrine of the knowledge of God, see Bruce McCormack, *Karl Barth's Critically Realistic Dialectical Theology: Its Genesis and Development, 1909–1936* (Oxford: Clarendon Press, 1995); Cornelis van der Kooi, *As in a Mirror: John Calvin and Karl Barth on Knowing God: A Diptych*, Studies in the History of Christian Traditions, trans. Donald Mader (Leiden: E. J. Brill, 2005).

8. Barth, *CD* I/1:133.

9. Ibid., 140.

10. Ibid., 141.

11. Ibid., 153.

12. Ibid., 149.

13. Ibid., 163.

14. Ibid., 164.

15. Ibid., 169; italics added.

16. Ibid., 176.

17. Ibid., 169.

18. Ibid., 184.

19. Ibid., 176; *KD* I/1:183.

20. Ibid., 175; italics added; *KD* I/1:182.

21. Ibid., 132; *KD* I/1:136.

22. T. F. Torrance offers a succinct and accurate description of Barth's position on this point: "God's self-revealing and self-giving 'for us and for our salvation' can never cease to be God in action, and can never be received or enjoyed apart from the Person and Action of the Giver, but only through personal encounter and communion with him" ("Karl Barth and Patristic Theology," in *Theology beyond Christendom: Essays on the Centenary of the Birth of Karl Barth May 10, 1886,* ed. John Thompson [Allison Park, PA: Pickwick Publications, 1986], 221).

23. Barth, *CD* I/1:119.

24. Ibid., 165.

25. Ibid.

26. Ibid., 168; *KD* I/1:174.

27. Ibid., 165.

28. Ibid., 173.

29. Ibid., 167.

30. On the indirect union of the divine and human natures in the person of the Son of God, see Heinrich Heppe, *Reformed Dogmatics: Set Out and Illustrated from the Sources,* ed. Ernst Bizer, trans. G. T. Thomson (London: George Allen & Unwin, 1950), 431ff.

31. Failure to understand how Barth conceptualizes the distinction between God and human beings within their mutual communion is a contributing factor behind the contradictory charges that Barth's theology is dualistic (in which case there would be no genuine union) and pantheistic (in which case there would be no genuine distinction). As a rather extreme example of the latter, Cornelius Van Til charged that Barth's teaching concerning "God's participation in all the limitations and sinfulness of creaturehood and man's participation in the very essence of God" reveals that for Barth "the Creator-creature distinction is virtually removed" (*Christianity and Barthianism* [Philadelphia: Presbyterian and Reformed Publishing Co., 1962], 470). Cf. Helmut Thielicke's charge that, for Barth, "In the strict sense, then, election and rejection are no longer a drama between God and us but an intra-trinitarian event, a drama in God (which formally reminds us once again of the spirit-monon in Hegel). . . . This history—to put it strongly—threatens to become a panentheistic movement which has the character of a monologue of God" (*Modern Faith and Thought,* trans. Geoffrey Bromiley [Grand Rapids: Wm. B. Eerdmans Publishing Co., 1990], 404). The "monologue" charge is widespread. See, for example, Heinz Zahrnt, *The Question of God,* trans. R. A. Wilson (New York: Harcourt, Brace & World, 1969), 112; Alister E. McGrath, *The Making of Modern German Christology: From the Enlightenment to Pannenberg* (Oxford: Oxford University Press, 1986), 106; Philip J. Rosato, *The Spirit as Lord: The Pneumatology of Karl Barth* (Edinburgh: T. & T. Clark, 1981), 141.

32. For example, R. H. Roberts writes: "Like some cancerous Doppelgänger, theological reality appears to inflate itself, drawing life from the reality it condemns, perfecting in exquisite form what could be seen as the most profound and systematically consistent theological alienation of the natural order ever achieved" ("Karl

Barth's Doctrine of Time: Its Nature and Implications," in *Karl Barth: Studies of His Theological Method*, ed. S. W. Sykes [New York: Oxford University Press, 1979], 124–25); Robert E. Willis writes: "There does indeed appear to be operative in Barth's anthropology, if not a final or remedial 'absorption' of the human, at least a serious ambiguity about its status. Where the question of man's status as ethical subject and agent is at stake, however, any ambiguity may prove fatal" (*The Ethics of Karl Barth* [Leiden: E. J. Brill, 1971], 445); Heinz Zahrnt asks: "How can anything still happen when everything has already 'happened' in eternity?" (*The Question of God*, 113). The best responses to this standard criticism are George Hunsinger's *How to Read Karl Barth* and John Webster's *Barth's Ethics of Reconciliation* and *Barth's Moral Theology*. See also Archibald Spencer's *Clearing a Space for Human Action: Ethical Ontology in the Theology of Karl Barth* (New York: Peter Lang, 2003).

33. Barth, *CD* I/1:242.

34. Ibid., 246.

35. Ibid., 238; *KD* I/1:250; italics added.

36. Ibid., 194.

37. Ibid., 142.

38. This is the basis of Barth's rejection of all forms of "Cartesian" theology, which he understands as any method of theological investigation that takes as its starting point, and uses as its norm, some aspect of the inner constitution of human being, and in so doing substitutes a human word for the Word of God.

39. Ibid., 212.

40. Ibid., 220; italics added.

41. Ibid.

42. Ibid., 240.

43. Ibid., 246.

44. Ibid., 241.

45. Ibid.; *KD* I/1:254.

46. Barth's account of human knowledge of God and faith in paragraph six is everywhere imbued with his characteristic "actualism," which George Hunsinger describes as "the most distinctive and perhaps the most difficult of the motifs [in Barth's theology]. It is present whenever Barth speaks, as he constantly does, in the language of occurrence, happening, event, history, decisions, and act. At the most general level it means that he thinks primarily in terms of events and relationships rather than monadic or self-contained substances. So pervasive is this motif that Barth's whole theology might well be described as a theology of active relations. God and humanity are both defined in fundamentally actualistic terms" (*How to Read Karl Barth*, 30); see also *CD* II/1:257–72. For more on this theme in Barth's work, see David H. Kelsey, *The Uses of Scripture in Recent Theology* (Philadelphia: Fortress Press, 1975), 39–50; Jay Wesley Richards, *The Untamed God: A Philosophical Exploration of Divine Perfection, Immutability, and Simplicity* (Downers Grove, IL: Inter-Varsity Press, 2003), 106–51; Paul M. Collins, *Trinitarian Theology, West and East: Karl Barth, The Cappadocian Fathers, and John Zizioulas* (Oxford: Oxford University Press, 2001), esp. 89–101.

Throughout this study, I use the adjective "actualistic" to describe Barth's ontology of divine and human being, and I do so knowing full well that the term is problematic. Its great weakness is its potential to convey the mistaken impression that Barth has worked out a formal philosophical ontology independently of the material content of dogmatics. In truth, Barth's mature understanding of divine and human being arises from his dogmatic reflections—particularly his thinking concerning election and Christology. Barth's reflection on these matters led him away from traditional notions of being as "essence" fully describable apart from act to a conception of being in-act. For Barth, God's being is in-act, and the act in which God has his being is not just any act, but a particular one, the covenant that he has freely and graciously chosen and enacted for himself and humanity. Thus, "covenant ontology," a term whose origin is unclear, but which can be found, among other places, in the work of Bruce McCormack and David Willis, is a better name for Barth's ontology (McCormack, "Grace and Being: The Role of God's Gracious Election in Karl Barth's Theological Ontology," in *The Cambridge Companion to Karl Barth*, ed. J. B. Webster [New York: Cambridge University Press, 2000], 99; Willis, *Notes on the Holiness of God* [Grand Rapids: Wm. B. Eerdmans Publishing Co., 2002], 73). Nevertheless, I retain the term "actualistic," despite its limitations, because it immediately draws the reader's attention to the idea that being does not merely precede act, but is in-act, something that terms like covenantal and historical (as precisely defined by Barth) perhaps do not. In any event, the term cannot be wholly misleading, since Barth himself used it (e.g., *CD* IV/2:105; *KD* IV/2:116). See Barth's comments on the matter in his letter to Bultmann (Karl Barth to Rudolf Bultmann, 12 June 1928, in *Karl Barth/Rudolf Bultmann Letters 1922–1966*, ed. Bernd Jaspert and Geoffrey Bromiley, trans. Geoffrey Bromiley [Grand Rapids: Wm. B. Eerdmans Publishing Co., 1981], 40–42).

47. Barth, *CD* I/1:193; *KD* I/1:201.

48. Ibid., 194; *KD* I/1:202.

49. Cf. van der Kooi's telling observation: "For Barth 'noetic' is not the same as having only intellectual knowledge of something. Anyone who learns to know Jesus Christ as the Yes of God discovers how much his own existence in fact contradicts this. I propose that at this point there has not been even a beginning made in digesting Barth's theology" (*As in a Mirror*, 413).

50. The term "existential" here does not, of course, describe a method of theological inquiry. Barth is clear that "even the transition to 'existential' thinking does not help us" (*CD* I/1:222). Speaking of Barth's Christology in *CD* IV, John Webster writes: "On its own distinct grounds and in a very distinct sense, it is, in part at least, an 'existential' or 'moral' Christology" (*Barth's Ethics of Reconciliation*, 82). I use the term similarly, as a label for the thought articulated in the next quotation. Although Joseph L. Mangina's study proceeds along very different lines from mine and reaches interpretive conclusions that I do not share, it helpfully describes "the real, fully self-involving character of the knowledge of God," that Barth offers, and indeed Mangina asserts that, for Barth, "the Christian life is nothing less than a form of human participation in the life of God" (*Karl Barth on the Christian Life: The Practical Knowledge of God* [New York: Peter Lang, 2001], 5).

51. Barth, *CD* I/1:224, italics added; *KD* I/1:235: "Wir kennen sie dann, wenn wir sie nur noch bejahen können, weil wir selber in unserer ganzen Existenz ihre Verwirklichung sind."

52. Ibid., 204.

53. Ibid., 206.

54. Ibid., 200–201; *KD* I/1:209.

55. "Πίστις says more than γνῶσις, but in all circumstances it says γνῶσις too" (ibid., 229).

56. Ibid., 200.

57. Ibid.; *KD* I/1:208.

58. Ibid., 207–8. For an excellent discussion of this point, see Hunsinger, *How to Read Karl Barth*, 185–224; see also Webster's comment that "we need to beware of presenting Barth as trapped within a competitive picture: either God's action or ours, either grace or history. For what Barth is denying is not that human action has any entitlement to exist, but that it can be considered as having self-evident status, on the basis of which we may proceed to erect some kind of assemblage of cultural forms, including notions of God. Barth's concern is not with the elimination of responsible human action, but with its placing or specification" (*Barth's Moral Theology*, 37–38).

59. Barth, *CD* I/1:240; *KD* I/1:253.

60. Ibid., 238; *KD* I/1: 251.

61. Ibid., 239.

62. Ibid., 236. Thus, Gary D. Badcock's claim that "Barth's theology is anything but private and subjective, but in this lies its weakness as well as its strength: it is quite simply incapable of sustaining any kind of spirituality theology" is true if and only if "spirituality" must be "private and subjective," which, of course, Barth denies (*The Way of Life: A Theology of Christian Vocation* [Grand Rapids: Wm. B. Eerdmans Publishing Co., 1998], 68).

63. Barth, *CD* I/1:240.

64. Ibid., 212.

65. Ibid., 237; italics added.

66. Ibid., 244.

67. See pp. 78–79.

68. Ibid., 222.

69. Ibid., 240.

70. Ibid.

71. Ibid., 238; *KD* I/1:251.

72. Ibid., 240.

73. Ibid.

74. Ibid. Later, in *CD* IV/2, when Barth takes up the Lutheran doctrine of the *communicatio idiomatum*, he will have revised this judgment. There Barth is able to see clearly that Luther's own theology, like that of the Eastern Church, entails deification.

75. Barth, *CD* I/1:239; *KD* I/1:252. Previously I pointed out that according to Barth, Augustine rejected the essential deification of the human. Two pages later, however, in the sentence just quoted, Barth qualifies this point. Against Pelagius, Augustine maintained the absolute priority of divine grace. Nevertheless, his description of this event, like that of the Lutheran Karl Holl after him, implies an essential deification of the human by dialectically identifying divine and human actions. According to Barth, "there can be no point in trying to maintain man's self-determination in some way, even dialectically, over against the determination of man by God. Precisely as self-determination, it is subject to determination by God. Our very self-determination needs this determination by God in order to be experience of His Word. In this relation of total subjection and need vis-a-vis determination by God it cannot possibly replace this, as Pelagius wished, or co-operate with it, as the Semi-Pelagians wished, or be secretly identical with it, as Augustine wished. Such solutions may be generally possible when reference is to other competing determinations of man or of an object, but here, where it is a matter of the determination of man by God and by himself, they are impossible" (ibid., 200).

76. Ibid., 220.
77. Cf. ibid., 238.
78. Ibid., 221.

CHAPTER 2

1. Barth, *CD* II/2:3.

2. Ibid., x. For more on Barth's doctrine of election, see Matthias Gockel, "One Word and All Is Saved: Barth and Schleiermacher on Election" (PhD diss., Princeton Theological Seminary, 2002); Bruce McCormack, "Grace and Being," 92–110; Colin Gunton, "The Doctrine of God: Karl Barth's Doctrine of Election as Part of His Doctrine of God," in *Theology through the Theologians: Selected Essays 1972–1995* (Edinburgh: T. & T. Clark, 1996), 88–104.

3. Barth, *CD* II/2:x; *KD* II/2:viii.

4. Ibid., 157.

5. Ibid., 3–34.

6. Ibid., 94–194.

7. Ibid., 3.

8. See Bruce McCormack, "Grace and Being," 92–110.

9. Barth, *CD* II/2:9; *KD* II/2:8; see also *CD* II/2:91 (*KD* II/2:98), where the same phrase is used.

10. Ibid., 6.

11. Ibid., 6; see also 52, 54. The ordering of election and Trinity in Barth's theology is the subject of significant current debate. See Paul D. Molnar, *Divine Freedom and the Doctrine of the Immanent Trinity: In Dialogue with Karl Barth and Contemporary Theology* (Edinburgh: T. & T. Clark, 2002); "The Trinity, Election and God's Ontological Freedom: A Response to Kevin W. Hector," *International Journal of Systematic Theology* 8 (2006): 294–306; Kevin Hector, "God's Triunity and Self-Determination: A Conversation with Karl Barth, Bruce McCormack and Paul Molnar," *International Journal of Systematic Theology* 7 (2005): 246–61; Edwin Chr. van Driel, "Karl Barth on the Eternal Existence of Jesus Christ," *Scottish Journal of Theology* 60, no. 1 (2007): 45–61; Bruce McCormack, "Grace and Being"; "Seek God Where He May Be Found: A Response to Edwin Chr. van Driel," *Scottish Journal of Theology* 60, no. 1 (2007): 62–79.

12. Eberhard Jüngel claims that for Barth, "Decision does not belong to the being of God as something supplementary to this being; rather, as event, God's being is his own decision. 'The fact that God's being is event, the event of God's act, necessarily . . . means that it is His own conscious, willed and executed decision' (2.1.271)" (*God's Being Is in Becoming*, 81); see also Robert Jenson's statement: "*God Himself decides what He shall be, what His nature shall be. . . . God is His own decision*" (*Alpha and Omega: A Study in the Theology of Karl Barth* [New York: Thomas Nelson & Sons, 1963], 70).

13. Barth, *CD* II/2:53.

14. Ibid., 8.

15. Ibid., 6.

16. Ibid., 92.

17. Ibid., 8.

18. Ibid., 58; *KD* II/2:62.

19. Ibid., 7; *KD* II/2:6.

20. Ibid.

21. F. W. Graf unambiguously states that in Barth's theology humanity has been "eliminated"; cited in Wolf Krötke, "The Humanity of the Human Person in Karl Barth's Anthropology," in *The Cambridge Companion to Karl Barth*, 164.

22. See Jung Suck Rhee, *Secularization and Sanctification: A Study of Karl Barth's Doctrine of Sanctification and Its Contextual Application to the Korean Church* (Amsterdam: VU University Press, 1995): "It is thus the 'eschatological orientation' or 'teleological direction' which is really distinctive in Barth's theology" (142). It goes without saying that Barth is not advocating teleology in general, but a very specifically oriented teleology, grounded in the living Lord Jesus Christ who was, who is, and who is to come.

23. Barth, *CD* II/2:19, italics added; *KD* II/2:19. Because he fails to appreciate this point, Helmut Thielicke claims that for Barth, "We no longer await anything for everything has already happened. Nothing can be consummated, for we already participate in the consummation" (*Modern Faith and Thought*, 405). Thielicke is denying that the first form of participation in Christ (the objective form) leaves any room for a genuine second form (the subjective form). Yet Barth's position is exactly the opposite. Since objective participation in Christ is a teleological reality, rather than eclipsing genuine human action, it actually guarantees it. The same criticism applies to Heinz Zahrnt's comment: "Barth's error lies in over stressing his Christological lever. The consequence is that he does not leave sufficient breathing space between the creation and the redemption, so that the reality of redemption overwhelms the reality of creation—nature, history, the world and man—like a tidal wave" (*The Question of God*, 105). See John Webster's comment: "Barth's apparent ontological exclusiveness is in fact an inclusivism: *solus Christus* embraces and does not suspend or absorb the world of creatures and their actions" (*Barth's Ethics of Reconciliation*, 29).

24. Barth, *CD* II/2:9; *KD* II/2:8.

25. Ibid., 10; *KD* II/2:9.

26. Ibid.

27. Ibid., 11.

28. Ibid., 30.

29. Ibid., 31; *KD* II/2:32: "Und das ist es, was das Geheimnis dieser Wahl für das Geschöpf bedeutet: daß es in die Ruhe versetzt wird. In die Ruhe der Entscheidung und des Gehorsams: denn es ist das Geheimnis des lebendigen und lebendigmachenden Gottes."

30. Barth's claim that the "rest" that human beings are given in Jesus Christ is not merely stillness, but rather ordered activity, is grounded in his understanding of the being of God. Cf. Eberhard Jüngel's statement: "The harmony of the triune God is thus not the harmony of a God at rest in himself, but the harmony of God's self-moved being. This harmony is rest as movement, not comparable to the peace of an unmoved mover. The fact that God rests in himself 'does not exclude but includes the fact that His being is decision' (II/2, 175)" (*God's Being Is in Becoming*, 88).

31. In chapter 5, I will show that Barth refuses to follow the dominant tradition within Christian theology, which conceives of grace as involving the infusion of virtues or habits within the soul of believers. This should come as no surprise given the conclusions of the first chapter, particularly Barth's affirmation of the *simul ius-*

tus et peccator dictum. Barth maintains his adherence to this dictum throughout the *Church Dogmatics*, and his position in *CD* II/2 is consistent with his later denial of infused habits. According to Barth, the certainty of election, the certainty of God's promise of the telos established for humanity in the election of Jesus Christ, provides all the constancy necessary for the Christian life. The concept of infused habits is a way of substantially accounting for concrete acts of obedience—the specific acts themselves proceeding from the habit infused in the soul. Moreover, the growth of such infused habits within the soul is the result of "progress" in the Christian life. Yet Barth is offering a completely different theological description of the source of Christian obedience. According to Barth, the ground of obedient human action is located in the objective reality of human being in Christ, and concrete acts of obedience are the fulfillment of the telos given to each and every human life in the election of Jesus Christ. That being the case, there is no need for the idea of infused habits. It is rendered superfluous as a concept. Barth does not conceive of "progress" in the Christian life as the acquisition or "growth" of infused virtues, but rather as an increase in the constancy with which the actions of one's life correspond to the truth of one's objective being in Christ. Barth, of course, agrees with a great deal of the valuable Christian writing on the subject of the virtues. What he disagrees with is the ontology that underlies most of this writing. In fact, alert readers will notice that throughout the *Church Dogmatics*, Barth translates many of these edifying and enduring insights into his own covenantal-historical framework.

32. Barth's refusal to specify the content of communion with each "person" of the Trinity, as, for example, John Owen does in his great work "Of Communion with God the Father, Son, and Holy Ghost, Each Person Distinctly, in Love, Grace and Consolation" (*The Works of John Owen*, 16 vols., ed. William H. Goold [Edinburgh: Banner of Truth Trust, 1965], vol. 2), can perhaps be traced back to his desire to emphasize this point.

33. Barth, *CD* II/2:101.

34. Ibid., 116.

35. Ibid., 116; *KD* II/2:125. See also pp. 98–99, where Barth argues that the deity of Jesus enables him to be the κεφαλή in whom revelation and reconciliation "can be only an ἀνακεφαλαιοῦσθαι of all things."

36. T. F. Torrance argues that Barth affirms the very thing that I am arguing he denies. Torrance describes Barth's position as follows: "Yet in appropriating our sinful and rebellious nature like that, instead of sinning himself, Christ did the very opposite, for by bringing the holiness and righteousness of God to bear upon it, he condemned sin in the flesh, and through his atoning self-offering and self-consecration in our place he healed, redeemed and sanctified in and through himself what he had assumed. It is supremely important to realize therefore and this is the thrust of Barth's position that in the very act of taking our fallen nature upon himself Christ was at work healing, redeeming and sanctifying it" ("Karl Barth and Patristic Theology," 230–31). There is an interesting parallel between Barth's position as I am interpreting it and Carolyn Schneider's claim that "Athanasius does not talk of our sharing a common humanity with Christ in the sense that we merely have attributes in common, nor does he talk of our sharing a common humanity with Christ in the sense that we share with Christ in some Form of humanity external to us both. Rather, Jesus himself is the Form of humanity who participates in nothing, but is participated in" ("The Intimate Connection between Christ and Christians in Athanasius," *Scottish Journal of Theology* 58, no. 1 [2005]:12).

37. Barth, *CD* II/2:117.
38. Ibid., 149.
39. Ibid.
40. Ibid., 153.
41. Ibid., 105.
42. Ibid., 122. Paul Fiddes claims that "Barth rejects any idea that Christ atones for our sin by bearing a punishment in our place. Rather by identifying himself with humankind in a representative way as 'the one great sinner,' Christ 'caused sin to be taken and killed on the cross in his own person'" (*Past Event and Present Salvation: The Christian Idea of Atonement* [London: Darton, Longman & Todd, 1989], 134). But why would being the representative of humanity preclude his suffering punishment in our place? According to Barth, Jesus Christ suffers the punishment which we deserve *because* he is our representative. His life and death in our place certainly involve more than just punishment, but they do include it. As Barth writes, in Jesus Christ: "God, has stepped into our place, suffering our punishment, but also receiving a reward— my punishment and my reward" (*CD* IV/2:582). Furthermore, Barth never outgrows this position. He affirms it throughout the volume on reconciliation. For example, "Because He is God He has and exercises the power as this man to suffer for us the consequence of our transgression, the wrath and *penalty* which necessarily fall on us, and in that way to satisfy Himself in our regard" (*CD* IV/1:12, italics added).
43. Barth, *CD* II/2:125.
44. Ibid., 515.
45. Ibid., 603.
46. Ibid., 518.
47. Ibid., 613.
48. On Barth's ethics in general, see Nigel Biggar, *The Hastening That Waits* (Oxford: Clarendon Press, 1993); John Webster, *Barth's Ethics of Reconciliation*; Robert E. Willis, *The Ethics of Karl Barth* (Leiden: E. J. Brill, 1971); David Clough, *Ethics in Crisis: Interpreting Barth's Ethics* (Aldershot: Ashgate, 2005).
49. Barth, *CD* II/2:567.
50. Ibid., 613; *KD* II/2:681.
51. Ibid., 609; *KD* II/2:677.
52. Ibid., 512.
53. Ibid., 517.
54. Ibid., 605; *KD* II/2:673.
55. Ibid.
56. Ibid., 562.
57. Ibid., 780; *KD* II/2:874.
58. Ibid., 708. Nigel Biggar observes that by "command" Barth means "an event of personal encounter between God and the human creature." Thus, Barth prefers the word command to that of law because "it does not denote a natural or conventional institution but rather a momentary utterance issued directly by one person to another" (*The Hastening That Waits*, 14).
59. Barth, *CD* II/2:709; *KD* II/2:791.
60. Ibid., 557. For more on gospel and law in Barth, including bibliographical references to the relevant literature, see Jüngel, *Karl Barth: A Theological Legacy*, 105–26; Busch, *The Great Passion*, 152–75; Sung Wook Chung, *Admiration and Challenge: Karl Barth's Theological Relationship with John Calvin* (New York: Peter Lang, 2002), 177–204.
61. Barth, *CD* II/2:601.

62. Ibid., 600.

63. Ibid., 601. Significantly, Barth's basic criticism of the Platonic conception of "a mutual *methexis* (or participation)" is that "within the framework of this transformation it is quite impossible to show any basis for a real divine claim or real human obedience" (ibid., 555). One can imagine Barth employing the same argument against the use of the category of "participation" in the work of a number of the theologians associated with "Radical Orthodoxy" (e.g., *Radical Orthodoxy: A New Theology*, ed. John Milbank, Catherine Pickstock, and Graham Ward [London: Routledge & Kegan Paul, 1999]). For more on Plato's conception of participation in the forms, see Christopher Stead, *Philosophy in Christian Antiquity* (Cambridge: Cambridge University Press, 1994); Charles P. Bigger, *Participation: A Platonic Inquiry* (Baton Rouge: Louisiana State University Press, 1968).

64. Ibid.

65. Ibid.

66. Ibid., revised.

67. Ibid., 512.

68. See also endnote 31 in this chapter.

69. Ibid., 645.

70. Ibid., 540; *KD* II/2:599–600.

71. Thus, the charge that Barth's ethics is "occasionalist" does not stick. If, as Barth puts it elsewhere, "the command of God secretly fills every moment of our lives" (*CD* II/2:612), then it is not issued only on certain occasions, but always. Furthermore, there is an inward continuity to each of the discrete commands that is issued, because each one of them is issued by Jesus Christ, who is always continuous with himself. As Nigel Biggar puts it: "The fact that each singular event of encounter between the commanding God and sinful human being is a moment in a history which is ordered by this definite intention of God [i.e., Jesus Christ] gives to each historically contingent divine command its *ratio* and raises it above the status of one element in a chaos of individual conflicting intimations to individual human beings in individual situations" (*The Hastening That Waits*, 28); David Clough makes essentially the same claim as Biggar in *Ethics in Crisis*, 126. For the charge of occasionalism, see James M. Gustafson, *Can Ethics Be Christian?* (Chicago: University of Chicago Press, 1975), 160.

72. Barth, *CD* II/2:611; *KD* II/2:680.

73. Ibid., 620; italics added.

74. Ibid., 624.

75. Ibid., 646.

76. Ibid., 647; *KD* II/2:721.

77. Ibid., 638.

CHAPTER 3

1. Karl Barth, *Church Dogmatics* III/2: *The Doctrine of Creation*, ed. G. W. Bromiley and T. F. Torrance, trans. H. Knight et al. (Edinburgh: T. & T. Clark, 1960), ix.

2. Ibid., 132.

3. Barth, *CD* II/2:48; *KD* II/2:51. For some reason the English translation omits the exclamation point. George Hunsinger labels this aspect of Barth's theology as "particularism"; see *How to Read Karl Barth*, 32ff.

4. Barth, *CD* II/2:x.

5. Karl Barth, *Church Dogmatics* III/1: *The Doctrine of Creation*, ed. G. W. Bromiley and T. F. Torrance, trans. J. W. Edwards et al. (Edinburgh: T. & T. Clark, 1958), 94ff.

6. *CD* III/2:132–202.

7. Barth, *CD* III/2: 132; *KD* III/2: 158. On Barth's theological anthropology, see Wolf Krötke, "The Humanity of the Human Person in Karl Barth's Anthropology"; Stuart D. McLean, *Humanity in the Thought of Karl Barth* (Edinburgh: T. & T. Clark, 1981); Eberhard Jüngel, *Karl Barth: A Theological Legacy*, 103–38; J. B. Webster, *Barth's Ethics of Reconciliation* and *Barth's Moral Theology*; Daniel J. Price, *Karl Barth's Anthropology in Light of Modern Thought* (Grand Rapids: Wm. B. Eerdmans Publishing Co., 2002).

8. Barth, *CD* III/2:135; *KD* III/2:162.

9. Ibid., 132.

10. Ibid., 133; *KD* III/2:159.

11. See John Webster's comment: "More than anything else, Barth wants to shake anthropology free from the assumptions that 'being in Christ' is merely one modulation of something more humanly basic, and that human history and activity can be understood without direct and immediate reference to the history and activity of Jesus Christ" ("Barth and Postmodern Anthropology," in *Karl Barth: A Future for Postmodern Theology?* ed. Geoff Thompson and Christiaan Mostert [Hindmarsh: Australian Theological Forum, 2000], 61).

12. Barth, *CD* III/2:143.

13. Ibid., 150; *KD* III/2:179.

14. Ibid.

15. Ibid., 151.

16. Ibid.

17. Ibid., 152.

18. Ibid., 140.

19. Ibid., 157.

20. Ibid., 158.

21. Ibid; *KD* III/2:189.

22. Ibid.

23. The German original lacks "dynamic movement," but the sense is correct: "Dieses Geschöpf ist, was es als Geschöpf ist, indem der Schöpfer zu ihm, indem es zum Schöpfer hin ist" (*KD* III/2:190).

24. Barth, *CD* III/2:159–60; *KD* III/2:190.

25. Patrick Patterson argues that Barth's theology is a corrective to both modern liberal Christology as well as much New Testament scholarship in that it affirms a patristic anhypostatic-enhypostatic Christology ("Chalcedon's Apprentice: Karl Barth and the Twentieth-Century Critique of Classical Christology," *Toronto Journal of Theology* 16, no. 2 [2000]: 193–216). Perhaps so, but by actualizing the hypostatic union, Barth's theology is also a corrective to patristic Christology.

26. Barth, *CD* III/2:157.

27. Ibid., 161.

28. Ibid., 159.

29. Ibid., 164.

30. Ibid.

31. Ibid.

32. Additionally, it would seem that one's own previous history, the sum total of one's previous actions, would, in a secondary sense, also underlie the identity of every individual person, although Barth does not make that point here.

33. See Robert Jenson's comment: "For a creature, to be is to be destined to be with God in Christ. Man's denial of God is therefore denial of himself" (*Alpha and Omega*, 41).

34. Barth, *CD* III/2:176.

35. Ibid.

36. Ibid., 177; *KD* III/2:211. Rather than "man is the context," the translation should read "is in the context," since, of course, the context includes God: "Der Mensch ist im Zusammenhang . . ." Nevertheless, the point the translator was trying to draw out is correct: humanity has its being in this context and not elsewhere.

37. Ibid., 178.

38. Ibid.

39. Ibid.

40. Ibid.

41. See pp. 100–101 n. 31.

42. Ibid., 179.

43. Ibid., 180; *KD* III/2:214.

44. Ibid., 181.

45. Ibid.

46. Ibid., 182.

47. Ibid., 186.

48. Ibid., 187; *KD* III/2:223.

49. Ibid, 191. In *CD* IV/4, Barth makes clear that the Christian life "is to be understood in its totality as a life in invocation of God" (*The Christian Life: Church Dogmatics* IV/4: *Lecture Fragments*, trans. Geoffrey Bromiley [Grand Rapids: Wm. B. Eerdmans Publishing Co., 1981], 49–50). God invites and commands human beings to pray, and in responding to this summons they actualize their freedom to live as God's covenant partners.

50. Barth, *CD* III/2:192.

51. Ibid., 194. According to Philip Rosato (*The Spirit as Lord*), Barth "robs man of a genuine role in either accepting or rejecting God's gracious activity on his behalf" by characterizing "the human response to the Spirit's gift of grace as something which is not proper to man himself" (142). "Barth's pneumatic ontology of man and of creation itself, because of its pure actualism and its relational character, seems to be 'tendentiously docetic'" (142). Rosato traces the deficiencies in Barth's anthropology back to the de jure–de facto framework: "The source of this serious flaw in Barth's theology . . . is once again the distinctions which he makes between the objective and the subjective, the ontic and the noetic, the *prius* and the *posterius*, the *illic* and the *hic*, the actual and the virtual, the *de jure*, and the *de facto*" (169). According to Rosato, Barth's denial of created grace, and his overblown Christology, leave no room for a meaningful de facto and constitute a denial of humanity itself. If human beings are real and free only in relation to Jesus Christ, then they are neither real nor free. Likewise, just as human nature can be real only if it exists in strict independence of Jesus Christ, the operation of the Spirit can only be real if it consists in a *new, independent*, and *supplemental* work to that of Christ's work. These three words constitute a refrain in Rosato's criticism of Barth. In Barth's theology, "the Spirit is deprived of an independent contribution to the process of salvation"

(158). "There is little attention paid to the possibility that the Holy Spirit could bring about new salvific events and that His definition as Revealedness and Historicity could be interpreted to mean that the Spirit supplements the revelation of the Word or that the Church, because of the Spirit's presence, can make up what is wanting in Christ" (163). In other words, since there is no room in Barth's theology for a meaningful de facto, the Spirit has nothing to do in the economy of salvation. Rosato concludes that "the role of the Spirit and of man is reduced to that of noetic and subjective compliance with the ontic and objective reality of Jesus Christ. In the end the Spirit and man are not, as Barth feared they might be, divorced from Christ; rather they are so linked to Him that an adequate distinction between them seems nebulous in the *Church Dogmatics*" (161).

To thoroughly respond to Rosato's criticism of Barth's anthropology would require a repetition of the contents of this study as a whole. But the question of whether Barth thinks that the Spirit effects something "new" in believers is an important one. And the answer would have to be, Yes and No. On the one hand, Jesus Christ's work is perfect, not partial, and requires no supplemental work of the Spirit. Jesus Christ has reconciled the world to himself, and therefore the transforming work of the Spirit proceeds teleologically from this objective fact and is never disconnected from it. On the other hand, the Spirit joins believers to Jesus Christ in time, an eschatological event in which human beings become something that they previously were not (in themselves). In Jesus Christ, the old humanity has been replaced with the new humanity, and the "new" work of the Spirit is to effect this transition in believers through faith and obedience. And as I have been arguing throughout this study, this work is *ontologically* significant. Rosato, of course, would be unsatisfied with this response, since he thinks that the Spirit's work is either independent of Jesus Christ's work or it is "only a transitory and superfluous office" (170). Yet Barth considered that kind of thinking to be a false disjunction.

52. Barth, *CD* III/2:196.

CHAPTER 4

1. Barth, *CD* IV/1:ix, 3.

2. Barth, *CD* IV/2:10.

3. Barth, *CD* IV/1:128.

4. For a treatment of the structural organization of Barth's doctrine of reconciliation, see Eberhard Busch, *Karl Barth: His Life from Letters and Autobiographical Texts,* trans. John Bowden (Grand Rapids: Wm. B. Eerdmans Publishing Co., 1976), 377–79.

5. Barth, *CD* IV/2:648.

6. Webster, *Barth's Ethics of Reconciliation,* 80.

7. For a helpful discussion of the Son's obedience, see John Thompson, *Christ in Perspective: Christological Perspectives in the Theology of Karl Barth* (Grand Rapids: Eerdmans, 1978), 58–60.

8. To round out the description of the whole, *CD* IV/2 treats reconciliation a second time under the heading "Jesus Christ, the Servant as Lord," and therefore accentuates the humanity of Jesus Christ; the kingly office; sin as sloth; sanctification; and love. In *CD* IV/3, "Jesus Christ, the True Witness," Barth treats reconcili-

ation a third time from the perspective of Jesus Christ in his divine-human unity, elaborating the prophetic office; sin as falsehood; vocation and Christian hope.

9. Barth, *CD* IV/1:3–21.

10. Ibid., 4; *KD* IV/1:3.

11. Ibid., 79–92.

12. Ibid., 92–122.

13. Ibid., 283–357.

14. Ibid., 286.

15. Ibid.

16. Ibid., 293.

17. Ibid.

18. Ibid., 317.

19. Ibid., 315.

20. Ibid., 34.

21. Ibid., 26.

22. Ibid., 44.

23. Ibid., 45; italics added.

24. Ibid., 50–51; italics added.

25. Ibid., 6.

26. Ibid.

27. Ibid; *KD* IV/1:5.

28. Ibid.

29. Ibid.; *KD* IV/1:6.

30. Barth, *CD* IV/1:8; *KD* IV/1:7.

31. Ibid.

32. Ibid., 12–13; *KD* IV/1:12.

33. This point leads Nigel Biggar to claim that Barth's theology "yields a notion of human freedom that is more apparent than real," since Barth thinks that "grace does not concede to the beloved the freedom to turn away permanently" (*The Hastening That Waits*, 5).

34. Colin Gunton, *The Christian Faith: An Introduction to Christian Doctrine* (Oxford: Basil Blackwell Publisher, 2002), 163.

35. Barth, *CD* IV/1:14.

36. Ibid.

37. Ibid.

38. Ibid., 15.

39. Ibid.

40. Ibid., 79.

41. Ibid., 81.

42. T. F. Torrance describes Barth's position as follows: "In Jesus Christ and in the Holy Spirit God freely gives himself to us in such a living personal way that the Gift and the Giver are one and the same, and cannot be detached from each other. As such Grace is not a transferable tangible state of the soul that can be possessed by us, or subjected to the control of the Church, any more than God himself, but must be continually given and received in living personal communion with God" ("Karl Barth and Patristic Theology," 222). Barth could hardly have put it better himself.

43. Barth, *CD* IV/1:83; *KD* IV/1:88. The German lacks the word "utter," yet the translation indicates the thought that Barth is trying to convey.

44. See especially Stanley Hauerwas, *Character and the Christian Life: A Study in Theological Ethics* (Notre Dame, IN: University of Notre Dame Press, 1997); Biggar, *The Hastening That Waits*, 127ff.

45. Barth, *CD* IV/1:84–88.

46. Ibid., 87.

47. Ibid., 85.

48. According to David Stubbs ("Sanctification as Participation in Christ"), Barth's doctrine of sanctification is a combination of Paul's notion of participation in Christ and Kant's epistemology and anthropology. Barth's Pauline and Kantian commitments collide with one another and destabilize his doctrine of sanctification, leading to a hybrid conception of participation in Christ: "Barth's mature theology of sanctification can be described as participation in Christ Kantian-style" (176). According to Stubbs, Barth's Kantianism negatively affects the material content of his doctrine of sanctification by leading him to deny "created grace." Barth, like Kant, views human beings as "points," and the result is a rather anemic doctrine of sanctification: for Barth "there is no creaturely 'form' of sanctification in the here and now" (27). Thus, Kant is responsible for Barth's denial of created grace, and the denial of created grace is proof of the inadequacy of Barth's doctrine of sanctification. Stubbs goes on to offer what he describes as "a better alternative for conceptualizing 'participation in Christ' and sanctification" than what Barth offers (435), and what he offers is a version of created grace. Yet Stubbs does not mention "The Grace of God in Jesus Christ." In fact, he gives no indication that he is aware of the detailed rationale that Barth gives in support of his rejection of created grace, an explanation driven entirely by the dogmatic assertion that grace is indivisible because Jesus Christ is indivisible. It is possible that Stubbs is correct that Barth's Kantian commitments are driving his rejection of created grace. If so, then Barth's dogmatic rationale would simply be a smokescreen hiding his real commitment to Kantian philosophy. But to persuasively support this claim, Stubbs would have to take up and address the material theological arguments that Barth makes in this section. Yet he does not mention them. That this crucial section would be entirely ignored in a work whose main constructive proposal is an argument for sanctifying grace is puzzling. Yet, throughout the work, Stubbs proves to be far more interested in uncovering the supposed hidden Kantian assumptions controlling Barth's doctrine of sanctification than he is in patiently attending to Barth's dogmatic arguments. The result is that Stubbs spends more time trying to discover and elucidate the philosophical framework within which Barth articulates his theology than he does actually interpreting Barth's texts. There is a certain irony to this. Stubbs's argument is that Kant's philosophy constitutes a straitjacket on Barth's theology. But equipped with this conviction, when Stubbs looks at Barth's theology, all he can see is Kant. Against Stubbs's depiction of Barth's anthropology, see Hans Urs von Balthasar's claim: "Barth does not mean to dissolve nature into a pointillist series of discrete and discontinuous momentary events, but to begin with the notion of 'fullest realization' and make that the standard and measure of the meaning and interpretation of being" (*The Theology of Karl Barth: Exposition and Interpretation*, trans. Edward T. Oakes, S.J. [San Francisco: Ignatius Press, 1992], 191).

49. Barth, *CD* IV/1:88.

50. Ibid.

51. Ibid., 89.

52. Ibid.; *KD* IV/1:95.

53. Ibid., 87.

54. Ibid., 84.

55. In this section, Barth uses the term "conversion" as an umbrella concept to describe the objective reconciliation of humanity with God in Jesus Christ. Almost exclusively, Barth does not employ the term conversion in its more normal usage as referring to the obedient response of individuals or groups of individuals to the gospel. Yet it would be a gross misunderstanding to conclude from this fact that conversion in the ordinary sense of the word has no place in Barth's theology or is simply replaced by the conversion of Jesus Christ. In fact, just the opposite is the case. The objective conversion of humanity to God does not render faith, love, and hope superfluous, but actually grounds and commands them as obedient expressions of submission to the truth. Thus, buried within his presentation, and almost as an aside, Barth acknowledges that there is a "special sense" in which "Christians and only Christians are converted to Him" (ibid., 148).

56. Ibid., 93; *KD* IV/1:99. For more on Barth's doctrine of justification, see Hans Küng, *Justification: The Doctrine of Karl Barth and a Catholic Reflection*, trans. Thomas Collins et al. (Camden, NJ: Thomas Nelson & Sons, 1964); Eberhard Jüngel, *Justification: The Heart of the Christian Faith*, trans. Jeffrey Cayzer (Edinburgh: T. & T. Clark, 2001); George Hunsinger, "A Tale of Two Simultaneities: Justification and Sanctification in Calvin and Barth," in *Conversing with Barth*, ed. Mike Higton and John C. McDowell (Aldershot: Ashgate, 2004), 68–89; Eberhard Busch, *The Great Passion*, 209ff.; Bruce McCormack, "Justitia Aliena: Karl Barth in Conversation with the Evangelical Doctrine of Imputed Righteousness," in *Justification in Perspective: Historical Developments and Contemporary Challenges*, ed. Bruce L. McCormack (Grand Rapids: Baker Academic, 2006), 167–96; Trevor A. Hart, *Regarding Karl Barth: Essays Towards a Reading of His Theology* (Exeter: Paternoster Press, 1999), 48–73.

57. Barth, *CD* IV/1:93.

58. Ibid.

59. Ibid., 93–94.

60. Ibid., 93.

61. Ibid., 94.

62. Ibid.; *KD* IV/1:100. According to Alister McGrath, for Barth "the theological drama which constitutes the Christian faith is thus held to concern man and his knowledge of God, rather than the salvation of sinful man, caught up in the cosmic conflict between God and sin, the world and the devil. Such a conflict is an impossibility within the context of Barth's theology, in that Barth shares with Hegel the difficulty of accommodating sin within an essentially monistic system. Barth has simply no concept of a divine engagement with the forces of sin and evil (unless these are understood in the epistemically reduced sense of 'ignorance' or 'misunderstanding'): instead, we find only talk about God making himself known to man" (*Iustitia Dei: A History of the Christian Doctrine of Justification*, vol. 2 [Cambridge: Cambridge University Press, 1986], 177). This statement is typical of McGrath's misleading treatment of Barth's understanding of justification in his well-known history of the doctrine. McGrath goes as far as to say that "Barth regards man's knowledge and insight, rather than God's activity, as forming the centre of theological reflection. Barth's entire discussion of the justification of man appears to refer to man's epistemic situation" (182). The inaccuracy of this statement will be readily apparent to anyone who has read the *Church Dogmatics*. As it turns out, McGrath is simply repeating Gustav Wingren's criticism of Barth (e.g., *Theology in*

Conflict: Nygren, Barth, Bultmann, trans. Eric Wahlstrom [Philadelphia: Muhlenberg Press, 1958]). Thus, what Robert Jenson writes concerning Wingren applies equally to McGrath: Wingren, according to Jenson, "constructs a 'Barth' who exists only in the pages of Wingren's books. This 'Barth' bears a crazy-mirror resemblance to the one from Basel. And Wingren's critique of this 'Barth' is often extremely acute— and thus has the same crazy resemblance to a genuine critique of the real Barth" (*Alpha and Omega,* 99).

63. Barth, *CD* IV/1:94.
64. Ibid.
65. Ibid., 94–95.
66. Ibid., 95.
67. Ibid.
68. Ibid.
69. Ibid., 93.
70. Ibid., 94.
71. Barth, *CD* IV/1:95; *KD* IV/1:102.
72. Ibid., 96.
73. Ibid., 97.
74. Ibid., 98.
75. Ibid., 99.
76. Ibid.; *KD* IV/1:107.
77. Ibid.
78. Ibid., 100. Given the quality and accuracy of Jung Suck Rhee's excellent study (*Secularization and Sanctification*), it is surprising to find him arguing that Barth "insisted that all men are sanctified *de jure* in the atoning death of Jesus. This contradicts the Calvinistic doctrine of the limited atonement and his universalistic statements are arbitrary and imaginative, contradicting even his own theology. However, it is noteworthy that the *de jure* sanctification is simply the divine offer of salvation and its legal basis while the factual (*de facto*) and real sanctification has to be appropriated by faith in the power of the Holy Spirit" (225). Throughout his study, Rhee correctly stresses the teleological character of sanctification. Yet he misses that the teleology is located precisely in the de jure, in Jesus Christ himself, and the command that he issues. Rhee rightly draws out that the sanctification of the community and the sanctification of the individual are not ends in themselves, but are teleologically directed toward the sanctification of the world: "the most distinctive perspective in Barth's doctrine of sanctification is 'teleological,' as he emphasizes that our individual sanctification is not an end in itself but rather its telos is the sanctification of the world, for which we are called as 'witnesses'" (226). Yet he does not see that for Barth de jure sanctification is more than an offer; it is a reality, and indeed a reality with teleological power oriented toward de facto sanctification.

79. Barth, *CD* IV/1:101.
80. Ibid., 99.
81. Ibid., 100; *KD* IV/1:110.
82. Ibid.
83. Ibid., 109.
84. Ibid., 111.
85. Ibid., 112.
86. Ibid.; *KD* IV/1:122.

87. Ibid.
88. Ibid., 104.
89. Ibid., 112.
90. Ibid., 113.
91. Ibid., 115.
92. Ibid., 119.
93. Ibid., 120.
94. Ibid., 8; *KD* IV/1:7.
95. Ibid., 125.
96. Ibid., 92.
97. Ibid., 527. With respect to its indispensability to the gospel, Barth can even say: "There never was and there never can be any true Christian Church without the doctrine of justification. In this sense it is indeed the *articulus stantis et cadentis ecclesiae*" (ibid., 523).

CHAPTER 5

1. Colm O'Grady, *An Introduction to the Theology of Karl Barth* (New York: Corpus Books, 1970), 2.
2. Barth, *CD* IV/2:105–6.
3. Ibid., 36; *KD* IV/2:38.
4. Ibid., 36–116.
5. Ibid., 511–33.
6. Barth, *CD* IV/3:520–54.
7. Barth, *CD* IV/2:104.
8. Ibid., 105; *KD* IV/2:116. The English translation tones down the sentence by leaving out the word "old." The German actually reads: "*Wir haben die alte Inkarnationslehre «aktualisiert» . . .*": "We have actualized the old doctrine of the incarnation."
9. Ibid., 106. "To his emphasis upon the *homoousion*, however, we must add the important place he gave to the Chalcedonian doctrine of the hypostatic union between the divine nature and the human nature in the one indivisible Person of Christ. It was impossible for Barth to agree with Harnack that the Chalcedonian formulation of the doctrine of Christ was an hellenisation of the Gospel through the irruption of Greek and in particular Aristotelian philosophical concepts into the understanding of the Church. While important Greek terms (*ousia, hypostasis, physis*, and the like) were taken over, their meaning was so radically altered that their new use actually helped to transform the very foundations of Greek thought and culture" (T. F. Torrance, "Karl Barth and Patristic Theology," 226–27). While this observation is correct, it must be added that just as the Fathers radically altered the meaning of these inherited terms, so too did Barth radically alter the meaning of the terms he inherited from the Fathers.
10. Ibid., 108.
11. Ibid.
12. Ibid., 109; *KD* IV/2:120–21.
13. Ibid., 108; *KD* IV/2:119.

14. Ibid., 109; *KD* IV/2:121. The English translation obscures the point Barth is making. The word translated "conjunction" is *Vereinigung*, Barth's ordinary word for "union," as in hypostatic union. Barth deliberately chose this word, rather than the alternative *Einheit*, to draw out the dynamic character of the hypostatic union. Indeed the word "union" perhaps does not even convey the dynamism, the livingness, which Barth thinks constitutes the history of the person Jesus Christ. Hypostatic "uniting" is closer to what he intended to convey—the emphasis being on the event itself rather than the result of the event. I will return to this point below.

15. Ibid., 115–16.

16. Ibid., 113.

17. Ibid., 107. This insight also led Barth to reject any sharp division between the states of humiliation and exaltation. In Barth's view, the tendency to hold these two at a distance is symptomatic of the same sort of static thinking that crippled the older teaching concerning the hypostatic union. According to Barth, humiliation and exaltation are not two "different and successive states," but "two opposed but strictly related moments in that history" (106). Overdrawing the distinction between the two states, Barth argues, robs Jesus Christ of his history and therefore of his being. "How could He be the living Jesus Christ if He were not the One He is in this movement [of simultaneous and unified humiliation and exaltation]?" (110).

18. According to Barth, the former includes the latter "in anticipation:" ". . . in anticipation His existence includes within itself our existence with Him" (*seine Existenz antizipierend unsere Existenz mit ihm in sich schließt*) (ibid., 342; *KD* IV/2:382).

19. Ibid., x; italics added.

20. Ibid., 19.

21. This seems the appropriate point at which to address the question of the impact that developments in Barth's Christology had on his understanding of participation in Christ. It is quite obvious that a shift of some kind has taken place within Barth's Christology between *CD* I/2 and *CD* IV/1. Whereas in *CD* I/2 Barth felt it necessary to offer a special doctrine of the person of Christ, by *CD* IV/1 he had become convinced that such a procedure was unfitting in light of the inseparability of the person and work of Christ. According to Bruce McCormack ("Barths grundsätzlicher Chalcedonismus?" *Zeitschrift für dialektische Theologie* 18 [2002]: 138–73), in the doctrine of election in *CD* II/2, the actualism that characterized Barth's understanding of the divine-human relation established in revelation was pushed back into the eternal being of God. Thus, Barth came to see more clearly that if the being of God and the person of Christ are constituted in the history of the covenant, then, at the very least, it becomes difficult to speak of a metaphysical "person" of Christ that exists above or apart from this history. That point, I think, is essentially correct. The question then becomes: What are the effects of this transition on the theme of participation in Christ as I have presented it in this study? The major difference between Barth's position as I presented it in the first chapter of this study (treating *CD* I/1) and that which he offers in *CD* II/2 and following is that in the latter volumes the objective aspect of participation is much more to the fore than it was in *CD* I/1. That is why my treatment of *CD* I/1 focused on de facto participation—the event of mutual indwelling. In *CD* I/1, Barth offered a decidedly actualistic conception of union with Christ in keeping with his actualistic construal of the event of revelation. Thus, since my presentation of Barth's understanding of participation in Christ has emphasized Barth's actualism from the very beginning, the shift in Christology (and anthropology as well) stemming from his doctrine of election has for

the most part gone unmentioned. Nevertheless, to the extent that Barth left behind the remnants of a substantialist divine ontology and replaced it with a Christology in which the being of God is *enacted* in the covenant of grace, Barth's assertion that human participation in the divine life just is the event of obedience in which human action corresponds to God's gracious action becomes even more plausible, since God's very being is now said to be constituted in the covenant of grace, the content of which is the history of God's fellowship with humanity.

22. Barth, *CD* IV/2:6; *KD* IV/2:4.

23. Ibid., 63; *KD* IV/2:67–68.

24. Ibid., 70–71; *KD* IV/2:76.

25. Ibid., 64. *Pace* Alar Laats who writes: "If the divine centre and the human centre of Christ are as close to each other as they are in Barth's later theology, then one is justified in expecting the acceptance by Barth of the concept of the *communicatio idiomatum*. But Barth does not do this. He consistently holds apart the divine and the human natures. Instead he identifies the divine and the human actions. The two centres are identical not on the level of being but on the level of act. This identity is not a state but a history" (Alar Laats, *Doctrines of the Trinity in Eastern and Western Theologies: A Study with Special Reference to K. Barth and V. Lossky* [Frankfurt: Peter Lang, 1999], 57). But for Barth the divine and human natures are not identical at all—much less "on the level of act." Instead, the divine and human natures *are* in the union and communion of Jesus Christ's divine and human actions.

26. Barth, *CD* IV/2:63.

27. Ibid., 64. Barth is clear throughout this paragraph that the incarnation does not involve a change in the divine essence, since the Son of God eternally elected to be the Son of Man. There is, however, an apparent contradiction in Barth's presentation regarding what happens to human essence when the Son of God becomes a man. Barth repeatedly says that the human essence assumed is not altered by this assumption. Yet the stated purpose of the paragraph is to affirm and describe the fact that human essence was indeed exalted and therefore transformed. This is not a real contradiction. In every place that Barth denies that human essence is changed, he is rejecting Docetism and affirming the *vere homo*, the truth that the Son of God really became a real man. In every place that Barth speaks of the transformation of human essence, its exaltation, he is speaking of the new humanity that the Son of God created by being the genuinely human being that he is.

28. Ibid., 70.

29. Ibid., 66.

30. Ibid.

31. Ibid., 69.

32. Ibid., 68.

33. In his essay "Karl Barth and Patristic Theology," T. F. Torrance does not mention the category of history. So when he writes that Barth's "Christology was thoroughly Patristic, both in its base and in its general orientation . . ." (226), the sentence would be correct if in place of "Patristic" Torrance had said "Reformed." For according to Barth himself, the basic impulse of his Christology is Reformed rather than Lutheran. Moreover, Barth links the Eastern Church's Christology with that of the Lutherans. Of course the Reformed were themselves deeply influenced by the church fathers, but the point remains that Barth's basic impulses were given to him by the Reformed—particularly their dynamic-covenantal emphasis.

34. Barth, *CD* IV/2:69.

35. See also pp. 12–14 and 43–45.
36. Ibid., 89.
37. Ibid., 72.
38. Ibid., 80.
39. Ibid., 89–90.
40. Ibid., 90. Joseph Mangina's *Karl Barth on the Christian Life* is a helpful study. Yet given the importance of the point now being investigated and the clarity with which Barth articulates it, it is surprising to find Mangina arguing that there is, after all, room in Barth's theology for the notion of *habitus*. According to Mangina, Barth "has richer resources for an ethics of character than he is usually given credit for" (xii), and while there is room within Barth's theology "for talk about dispositions and character . . . he generally failed to exploit the resources that were available to him" (7–8). An ethics of character would enable Barth to affirm the "continuity of the self's existence" (169), and the underlying assumption of Mangina's presentation is that apart from an ethics of character it would be impossible to do so. Thus, he attempts to show that there are in fact places in the posthumously published *Christian Life* where "it becomes fairly clear that the continuity and temporality of the agent as such is not really an issue for Barth. The zealous Christian is clearly a man or woman marked by a certain character" (184). The clear implication of this statement, as well as others like it, is that Mangina thinks that Barth finally came to see that his actualistic anthropology was a bit excessive and that he corrected it by moving toward an ethics of character.

There are at least two reasons why Mangina's position will not likely persuade those who have closely studied the relevant sections of the *Church Dogmatics*. The first is that nowhere in the *Church Dogmatics*, not even in *The Christian Life*, does Barth affirm anything like *habitus* as an acquired feature of the human being as such. And he certainly never came to regard it as a way of affirming "consistency and continuity in our lives as moral agents" (173). The examples that Mangina gives do not show otherwise. Given the fact that Barth adamantly, repeatedly, and for reasons crucial to his theology as a whole, rejects the idea of *habitus* throughout the *Church Dogmatics*, one is left with the impression that on this point Mangina is reading into Barth's theology what he would like to find there.

The second reason is that Mangina does not clearly explain the rationale behind Barth's rejection of *habitus*. In addition to not treating the crucial section in *CD* IV/1, "The Grace of God in Jesus Christ," he does not see that Barth's rejection of *habitus* is a *necessary* implication of his doctrines of election, Christology, anthropology, indeed of the whole drift of his actualistic portrayal of the covenantal relationship between God and human beings. In the absence of any detailed interaction with those major doctrines, Mangina presents his discovery of an ethics of character in Barth as a softening of Barth's previously unnecessary rejection of a useful concept. This claim will come across as entirely plausible to some of Mangina's readers. In truth, however, Barth's supposed move toward an ethics of character would have constituted a move away from the very heart of his theology—his covenantal-actualistic construal of God's relationship to the world in Jesus Christ.

41. Barth, *CD* IV/1:94; *KD* IV/2:104.
42. Ibid.
43. Ibid.
44. Ibid.
45. Ibid., 81.

46. Ibid., 82.
47. Ibid., 83.
48. Ibid., 69.
49. Ibid.
50. Ibid., 79; italics added. Commenting on *CD* IV/2, and particularly Barth's conception of *participatio Christi*, Rhee says this about Barth's doctrine of sanctification: "the exaltation of man does not even remotely imply some kind of 'deification' or 'divinization' of man" (*Secularization and Sanctification*, 155). Yet Barth is not merely rejecting deification, but taking up its central concern and addressing it within a wholly different framework. See also (ibid., 166–67), where Rhee presents Barth's position and deification as stark contrasts.
51. Barth, *CD* IV/2:77.
52. Ibid., 80.
53. Ibid., 77.
54. Ibid.
55. Ibid., 83.
56. Ibid., 91–92.
57. Ibid., 88.
58. Ibid., 89.
59. Ibid., 88.
60. Ibid.
61. Ibid.
62. Ibid.
63. Ibid., 19; *KD* IV/2:19.
64. Ibid., 107; *KD* IV/2:118.
65. Ibid., 96; *KD* IV/2:106.
66. Barth, *CD* IV/1:128; *KD* IV/1:140.
67. Barth, *CD* IV/2:49.
68. Ibid., 50.
69. Ibid., 102.
70. Ibid., 115.
71. Ibid.
72. Ibid.
73. Ibid., 86.
74. Ibid., 68.
75. Ibid., 70; italics added. In the last sentence of this quotation, Barth is arguing that Godhead as such does not assume flesh. Cf. the following statement: "Godhead as such has no existence. It is not real. It has no being or activity. It cannot, therefore, unite with that which is existent and real and has being and activity (which is not the case, of course, with human essence either). This is done by the divine Subject in and with His divine essence, by the One who exists and is and is actual, God the Father, Son and Holy Ghost, and therefore *in specie* God the Son. That is why it says that He, the Son, the Word became flesh. . . . He, the divine Subject, carries and determines the divine essence, and not conversely" (65).
76. According to Robert Jenson, "Barth's Christology is not so much a description of the individual person of Jesus Christ as it is a description of the history of God with man, of the one great event which is all of reality, at its personal center" (*Alpha and Omega*, 123). Jenson is certainly correct that Barth identifies Jesus Christ with his history, and that his history is not exclusive but inclusive. And yet would

it not have been preferable to say that Barth's Christology is a description of the inclusive *individual person* in whom "the history of God with man" occurs?

77. Barth, *CD* IV/2:90–91.

78. George Hunsinger, "Karl Barth's Christology: Its Basic Chalcedonian Character," in *Disruptive Grace*, 135; see also Charles T. Waldrop (*Karl Barth's Christology: Its Basic Alexandrian Character* [Berlin: Walter de Gruyter, 1984]).

79. The language is intentionally qualified because I am not attempting to make a historical evaluation of the factors that motivated the Antiochene theologians and their successors. If it could be shown that various Antiochene theologians do not fit this bill, then so be it. What matters is the dogmatic point that I am associating with them, since it is one that Barth was careful to avoid—whether or not it originated with or characterized the Antiochene theologians themselves.

80. Barth, *CD* IV/2:46–47. Richard Muller makes the following observation: "Barth does not cross the line from an essentially Reformed view of the union of the two natures to an essentially Lutheran view—and to that extent, recognizing the limitation of the language, we will have to classify him as Antiochene. Specifically, Barth does not accept the typically Lutheran (and Alexandrian!) view of the *communicatio idiomatum*, according to which attributes or properties of the divine person are communicated to and ultimately exercised in and by the human nature of Christ" ("Directions in the Study of Barth's Christology," *Westminster Theological Journal* 48 [1986]: 127). Muller is correct that Barth's Christology is inspired by Reformed rather than Lutheran or patristic Christology. He is also correct that Barth's understanding of the *communicatio idiomatum* is unlike the Lutherans and thus, in that sense, is closer to the Antiochene and Reformed concern. But to classify Barth's Christology as Antiochene could easily become misleading, for as I understand the original disputes the basic issue dividing the Antiochene and Alexandrian theologians concerned the question of whether or not Jesus Christ was one acting subject or two, and when Barth takes up that question, *mutatis mutandis*, he is altogether "Alexandrian."

81. Barth, *CD* IV/2:49.

82. There is a noticeable progression to Barth's thought on this matter. In *CD* II/1 he asserts that human fellowship with God is grounded in God's own fellowship with himself: God "does not exist in solitude but in fellowship. Therefore what He seeks and creates between Himself and us is in fact nothing else but what He wills and completes and therefore is in Himself" (275). In *CD* II/2 he elaborates on the nature of this fellowship when he writes, "In the beginning it was the choice of the Father Himself to establish the covenant with man by giving up His Son for him, that He Himself might become man in the fulfillment of His grace. In the beginning it was the choice of the Son to be obedient to grace, and therefore to offer up Himself and to become man in order that this covenant might be made a reality" (101). In *CD* IV/1 Barth fully embraces the implications of this line of thought: "We have not only not to deny but actually to affirm and understand as essential to the being of God the offensive fact that there is in God Himself an above and a below, a *prius* and a *posterius*, a superiority and a subordination" (200). "In the relationship of the Son to the Father (the model of all that is demanded from man by God), there is a pure obedience, subordination and subjection" (304). Indeed "His divine unity consists in the fact that in Himself He is both the One who is obeyed and Another who obeys" (201). Thus, since participation in Christ is participation in the Son's history of divine-human obedience, the fitting mode of its occurrence is human obedience

analogous to the Son's divine-human obedience. Along with the point made in chapter 2 regarding election and the being of God, this is the most important way in which Barth's doctrine of the Trinity shapes his understanding of participation in Christ.

83. Ibid., 511.

84. Barth, *CD* IV/1:138. Moreover, Barth adds that the Enlightenment treatment of the prophetic office had "practically nothing in common with the biblical concept of prophecy."

85. Ibid., 136.

86. Ibid.

87. Ibid.

88. Barth, *CD* IV/3.1:46.

89. Ibid., 280.

90. For an excellent discussion of this material, see John Webster, "Eloquent and Radiant: The Prophetic Office of Christ and the Mission of the Church," in *Barth's Moral Theology*, 125–50.

91. Barth, *CD* IV/3.2:520–54.

92. Ibid., 520.

93. Ibid., 521.

94. Ibid., 527.

95. Ibid., 530.

96. Ibid., 533.

97. Ibid., 534.

98. Ibid., 535.

99. Ibid.; *KD* IV/3.2:615.

100. Ibid., 535.

101. Ibid., 544.

102. Ibid., 538; *KD* IV/3.2:618.

103. *Pace* Gary Badcock's claim: "There is no suggestion that any sense of self-fulfillment or self-realization can legitimately enter into the discussion or that a free human response to God is what is in question. Rather, throughout the treatment of vocation, Barth focuses on the objective event by which humanity is set in the light of life" (*The Way of Life*, 57). The following charge is also false: "Nevertheless, there are major weaknesses in Barth's treatment of vocation, stemming from the problem that has already been highlighted: the lack of adequate attention to the structure of human life 'in Christ'" (68). Badcock could be correct that Barth's doctrine of vocation is inadequate, but if he were, he would have to provide reasons why. For the reason is certainly not that Barth fails to elucidate the shape of life in Christ. Of course, if by "structure" Badcock means a structural feature of humanity that is the ready soil for the work of the Spirit, then he is correct that Barth does not give "adequate attention" to that—Barth denies it. This denial, Badcock claims, reveals "a sense of subtlety in theological anthropology that is entirely absent from the Barthian approach, and which it badly needs" (69). Barth's theological anthropology might finally be wrong or in need of serious revision, but to suggest that it ham-handedly lacks subtlety does not count as a serious criticism.

104. *CD* IV/3.2:536.

105. Ibid.

106. Ibid.

107. Ibid.

108. Ibid.
109. Ibid.
110. Ibid., 540; *KD* IV/3.2:620.
111. Ibid.
112. Ibid., 540; see Albert Schweitzer, *The Mysticism of Paul the Apostle*, trans. William Montgomery (Baltimore: Johns Hopkins University Press, 1998).
113. Barth, *CD* IV/3.2:540.
114. Ibid.; *KD* IV/3.2:621: *"Es werden und sind Christus und der Christ in solcher Hingabe ein Ganzes, Eines, eine in sich differenzierte und bewegte, aber echte, solide Einheit."*
115. Ibid., 543.
116. Ibid., 598.
117. Barth, *CD* IV/2:106.
118. *KD* IV/1:213.
119. *CD* II/2:709; *KD* II/2:791.

CONCLUSION

1. See Kimlyn Bender's observation that the "relationship between Christ and the individual Christian is for Barth based upon the same patterns as that between Christ and the community. Barth refers to the union of Christ and the community as the *totus Christus*; he refers to the union of Christ and the believer as a *unio cum Christo*, a union with Christ. . . . Barth sees the relationship between Christ and the Christian, like that between Christ and the community, as predicated upon the unique relationship between the Word and flesh of Christ" (*Karl Barth's Christological Ecclesiology* [Aldershot: Ashgate, 2005], 203, n.12).

2. Within current Barth scholarship, the issue of "ecclesial mediation" figures prominently. Central to this discussion is the assessment of the adequacy of Barth's construal of the relationship between divine and human action, particularly his conceptualization of the status of church practices within the economy of grace. See, for example, John Yocum, *Ecclesial Mediation in Karl Barth* (Aldershot: Ashgate, 2004); Reinhard Hütter, "Karl Barth's 'Dialectical Catholicity': Sic et Non," *Modern Theology* 16, no. 2 (April 2000): 137–57; idem, *Suffering Divine Things: Theology as Church Practice* (Grand Rapids: Eerdmans, 2000); George Hunsinger, "Baptism and the Soteriology of Forgiveness," *International Journal of Systematic Theology* 2, no. 3 (2000): 247–69; Webster, *Barth's Ethics of Reconciliation*, esp. 117ff. On Barth's ecclesiology in general, see Colm O'Grady, *The Church in Catholic Theology: Dialogue with Karl Barth* (Washington-Cleveland: Corpus Books, 1969); and Kimlyn Bender, *Karl Barth's Christological Ecclesiology*.

3. Karl Barth, *Church Dogmatics* IV/4: *The Doctrine of Reconciliation: Baptism as the Foundation of the Christian Life* (Fragment), ed. G. W. Bromiley and T. F. Torrance, trans. G.W. Bromiley (Edinburgh: T. & T. Clark, 1969).
4. Ibid., 21.
5. Ibid., 14.
6. Ibid., 21.
7. Ibid., 22–23.
8. Ibid., 19.

9. Ibid.

10. Ibid., 25. See also pp. 41–42 where I briefly treat "The Verdict of the Father" (*CD* IV/1:283–357).

11. Ibid., 27.

12. Ibid., 29.

13. For a positive and negative assessment of Barth's pneumatology respectively, see George Hunsinger, "The Mediator of Communion: Karl Barth's Doctrine of the Holy Spirit," in *The Cambridge Companion to Karl Barth*, 177–94; Robert Jenson, "You Wonder Where the Spirit Went: Binitarian Tendencies in Barth's Theology," in *Pro ecclesia* 2 (1993): 296–304.

14. Barth, *CD* IV/4:30.

15. Ibid., 32.

16. Ibid., 34.

17. Ibid., 31.

18. Ibid., 33.

19. Ibid., 32.

20. See Cornelis van der Kooi's claim: "The doctrine of baptism is no alien element, but a ripe harvest of Barth's theology" (*As in a Mirror: John Calvin and Karl Barth on Knowing God*, 391). Cf. John Yocum who argues that Barth's position "subverts" earlier elements of his theology (*Ecclesial Mediation in Barth*, xi).

21. In *CD* IV/1, Barth provocatively diagnoses Bultmann's view as having its roots in a Roman Catholic error. He writes, "What is Bultmann's conception but an existentialist translation of the sacramentalist teaching of the Roman Church, according to which, at the climax of the mass, with the transubstantiation of the elements—in metaphysical identity with what took place then and there—there is a 'bloodless repetition' of the sacrifice of Christ on Golgotha?" (767).

22. Obviously, space prohibits me from exploring what such a view might look like. I should note, however, that this is a controversial point in the literature. For example, John Yocum (*Ecclesial Mediation in Barth*) and George Hunsinger (e.g., "Baptism and the Soteriology of Forgiveness," *International Journal of Systematic Theology* 2 [2000]: 247–69) think it is possible to construct such a position, while Eberhard Jüngel ("Karl Barths Lehre von der Taufe," in *Barth-Studien* [Zurich, Cologne, and Gütersloh: Benziger, 1982], 246–90) and Kurt Anders Richardson (*Reading Karl Barth*) think it isn't.

23. Barth, *CD* IV/2:572.

24. Ibid., 575.

25. Ibid., 573.

26. Ibid., 528.

27. Cf. Calvin's comment that "there never existed any work of a godly man which, if examined by God's stern judgment, would not deserve condemnation" (*Institutes of the Christian Religion*, ed. John T. McNeill, trans. Ford Lewis Battles, Library of Christian Classics [Philadelphia: Westminster Press, 1960], 21:778).

28. Barth, *CD* IV/2:528.

29. Ibid., 529.

30. The Greek word *theosis* is often translated "divinization." The more common term in patristic literature is *theopoiesis*, usually translated "deification." See David Balas, "Divinization," in *Encyclopedia of Early Christianity*, ed. Everett Ferguson (New York: Garland, 1997), 338–39. See also Basil Studer's helpful entry, "Divinization," *Encyclopedia of the Early Church*, ed. Angelo di Berardina (New York: Oxford

University Press, 1992), vol. 1, 242–43. On deification in the patristic period, the two best sources are Jules Gross, *The Divinization of the Christian According to the Greek Fathers*, trans. Paul Onica (Anaheim, CA: A & C Press, 2002), and Norman Russell, *The Doctrine of Deification in the Greek Patristic Tradition*, Oxford Early Christian Studies (New York: Oxford University Press, 2004); see also Basil Studer, *Trinity and Incarnation: The Faith of the Early Church*, ed. Andrew Louth, trans. Matthias Westerhoff (Collegeville, MN: Liturgical Press, 1993). For treatments of the theme within Eastern Orthodoxy, see John Meyendorff, *Byzantine Theology: Historical Trends and Doctrinal Themes*, 2nd ed. (New York: Fordham University Press, 1983); Kallistos Ware, *The Orthodox Church*, rev. ed. (New York: Penguin Books, 1993); Vladimir Lossky, *The Mystical Theology of the Eastern Church* (Crestwood, NY: St. Vladimir's Seminary Press, 1976), esp. chap. 10, titled "The Way of Union"; Panayiotis Nellas, *Deification in Christ: Orthodox Perspectives on the Nature of the Human Person*, trans. Norman Russell (Crestwood, NY: St. Vladimir's Seminary Press, 1987); Aristotle Papanikolaou, *Being with God: Trinity, Apophaticism, and Divine-Human Communion* (Notre Dame, IN: Notre Dame University Press, 2006).

31. This is the formulation of the Romanian theologian, and former executive secretary for mission and relations with Orthodox churches within the World Council of Churches, Ion Bria, quoted in Emil Bartos, *Deification in Eastern Orthodox Theology: An Evaluation and Critique of the Theology of Dumitru Staniloae* (Exeter: Paternoster Press, 1999), 7. Similar statements abound in the relevant literature.

32. Carl Braaten and Robert Jenson, eds., *Union with Christ: The New Finnish Interpretation of Luther* (Grand Rapids: Eerdmans, 1998); Tuomo Mannerma, "Theosis as a Subject of Finnish Luther Research," *Pro ecclesia* 4 (1995): 37–47; John Meyendorff and Robert Tobias, eds., *Salvation in Christ: A Lutheran-Orthodox Dialogue* (Minneapolis: Augsburg, 1992). For a history and analysis of this dialogue, see Risto Saarinen, *Faith and Holiness: Lutheran-Orthodox Dialogue, 1959–1994*, Kirche und Konfession, Bd. 40 (Gottingen: Vandenhoeck & Ruprecht, 1997); see also Hannu T. Kamppuri, *Dialogue between Neighbours: The Theological Conversations between the Evangelical-Lutheran Church of Finland and the Russian Orthodox Church, 1970–1986: Communiques and Theses* (Helsinki: Vammalan, 1986). In his recent essay "Luther's Contemporary Theological Significance," in *The Cambridge Companion to Martin Luther* (Cambridge: Cambridge University Press, 2003), Robert Jenson lists Luther's teaching concerning *theosis* as one of the areas in which he is most significant to contemporary theology.

33. John Meyendorff and Joseph C. McLelland, *The New Man: An Orthodox and Reformed Dialogue* (New Brunswick, NJ: Agora Books, 1973); Thomas Forsyth Torrance, ed., *Theological Dialogue between Orthodox and Reformed Churches*, 2 vols. (Edinburgh: Scottish Academic Press, 1985).

34. *Anglican-Orthodox Dialogue: The Moscow Statement Agreed by the Anglican-Orthodox Joint Doctrinal Commission, 1976: With Introductory and Supporting Material*, ed. Kallistos Ware and Colin Davey (London: SPCK, 1977).

35. The results of the Finnish interpretation of Luther are detectable in the Lutheran World Federation and the Catholic Church, *Joint Declaration on the Doctrine of Justification* (Grand Rapids: Eerdmans, 2000).

36. This claim will be obvious to any observer of the contemporary theological scene. Therefore I will not attempt to offer anything like an exhaustive bibliography of this material. Instead I will simply list one work apiece in which an influ-

ential theological figure within a particular Christian tradition (or, in Augustine's case, across traditions) is said to teach deification. In addition to the studies on Luther already mentioned, deification is also found in Thomas Aquinas—A. N. Williams, *The Ground of Union: Deification in Aquinas and Palamas* (New York: Oxford University Press, 1999); Augustine—Gerald Bonner, "Augustine's Conception of Deification," *Journal of Theological Studies*, n.s. 37, no. 2 (1986): 369–86; John Calvin—Carl Mosser, "The Greatest Possible Blessing: Calvin and Deification," *Scottish Journal of Theology* 55, no. 2 (2002): 36–57; and John Wesley—Michael Christensen, "Theosis and Sanctification: John Wesley's Reformulation of a Patristic Doctrine," *Wesleyan Theological Journal* 31, no. 2 (1996): 71–94.

37. Impediments to this recognition have come from both Eastern and Western theologians alike. On the one hand, in their desire to distance themselves from the many perceived errors of the Western tradition, Eastern theologians have been slow to acknowledge the presence of significant overlapping concerns in the realm of *theosis* between themselves and many Western theologians. This, for example, is evident even in someone with the ecumenical sensibilities of John Meyendorff, who, within the first four pages of his excellent work *Byzantine Theology*, claims that "the dynamism of Byzantine anthropology can easily be contrasted with the static categories of 'nature' and 'grace' which dominated the thought of post-Augustinian Western Christianity" (2). Meyendorff also claims that the affirmation of the orientation of human nature "to share in the divine life" is the "consensus which distinguishes Byzantine theology, taken as a whole, from the post-Augustinian and Scholastic West" (4). On the other hand, Adolf von Harnack is largely responsible for the Western slowness in perceiving this overlap. For example, he describes deification as a "severely Greek idea," and he states that "the notion of the redemption as a deification of mortal nature is subchristian" (*What Is Christianity?* trans. Thomas Bailey Saunders [Gloucester, MA: Peter Smith, 1978], 232, 235). Basil Studer faults Albrecht Ritschl: "Unfortunately [divinization's] consideration by Ritschl and his followers as, together with sacramentalism, a typical case of Hellenization of the gospel means that to this day its study has been compromised by more or less partial debates on certain unilateral premises" ("Divinization," 242).

38. Williams, *Ground of Union*, 32.

39. Studer, "Divinization," 242.

40. Jules Gross, *The Divinization of the Christian*, 272. Even Norman Russell's list of the variety of referents for the term deification should be understood as suggestive rather than exhaustive. He writes: "Deification is expressed through a number of different images: it is God's honoring of Christians with the title of 'gods'; it is the believer's filial adoption through baptism; it is the attaining of likeness to God through gnosis and dispassion; it is the ascent of the soul to God; it is the participation of the soul in the divine attributes of immortality and incorruption; it is the transformation of human nature by divine action; it is the eschatological glorification of both soul and body; it is the union with God through participation in the divine energies"; quoted in Bartos, *Deification in Eastern Orthodox Theology*, 10.

41. Gross, ibid.

42. Karl Barth, *Church Dogmatics* IV/1: *The Doctrine of Reconciliation*, ed. G. W. Bromiley and T. F. Torrance, trans. G. W. Bromiley (Edinburgh: T. & T. Clark, 1956), 8; *KD* IV/1:7.

43. See also pp. 12–14, 43–45, 65–69.

44. John Meyendorff writes: "The grace of deification, granted potentially in baptism, accepted freely and progressively throughout the whole course of life, leads us to vision and union" (*Saint Gregory of Palamas and Orthodox Spirituality*, trans. Adele Fiske [New York: St. Vladimir's Press, 1974], 40). Speaking of Gregory of Palamas, Meyendorff writes: "The end of the hesychast life was for him, as for all others, essentially the same as that set before all Christians by the Scriptures: to become conscious of the grace of baptism, already granted to man but hidden from him by sin" (ibid., 66). According to Dumitru Staniloae, the "graces of the mysteries [or sacraments] are fundamental operations performed by the Spirit in all people for their salvation, operations that are imprinted in them as powers" (quoted in Bartos, *Deification in Eastern Orthodoxy Theology*, 285). Bartos then goes on to note that according to Staniloae, "The Holy Spirit uses these graces to unite man and Christ, a union that is possible since 'at the beginning of all gifts there is one grace received through a mystery [that is, a sacrament]'" (ibid.). Gross, at the end of his study of deification in the patristic period, draws the following important conclusion: "Saint Irenaeus already taught—and was followed in this from the fourth century by all the Greeks—that the Holy Spirit is present in the Christian not only by His virtue, but by His essence. Basil and Cyril of Alexandria are particularly definite on this point. Moreover, the latter two doctors imply clearly enough that the divine Dweller, not content to dwell in the righteous soul substantially, becomes, as it were, its 'form' and produces in it a 'quality' which assimilates it to Christ. In this 'divine conformation,' which seems like a created grace, distinct but inseparable from the Holy Spirit, *we may well recognize our habitual or sanctifying grace*" (Gross, *The Divinization of the Christian*, 270, italics added). Barth's rejection of any sort of mediating grace or habit constitutes a departure not only from Roman Catholicism and Orthodoxy, but from virtually everyone else as well. To take an example from his own Reformed tradition, according to John Owen, the Holy Spirit, by virtue of our union with Christ, communicates a substantive principle of life to the individual soul which it lacks because of its sin: "[I]n the sanctification of believers, the Holy Ghost doth work in them, in their whole souls, their minds, their wills, and affections, a gracious, supernatural habit, principle, and disposition of living unto God; wherein the substance or essence, the life and being, of holiness doth consist" (John Owen, *The Works of John Owen*, 16 vols., ed. William H. Goold [Edinburgh: Banner of Truth Trust, 1965], vol. 3, 469). Owen specifically contrasts this principle with the acts of obedience that arise from it, whereas Barth conceives of our acts of obedience as the very content of our subjective union with Christ. For Owen, habits are necessary to guarantee that regeneration is "real," whereas for Barth, the reality of our subjective union with Christ just is these acts in which human beings become who they already objectively are in Christ.

45. Meyendorff, *Byzantine Theology*, 226.

46. What Gross says of Irenaeus could serve as a description of the rest of subsequent Orthodoxy: "As precious as it may be, the gift of the divine ὁμοίωσις granted to the Christian from the time of this life onward is only a seed. Even though it develops in advance here below, it will only blossom in full in the hereafter" (*The Divinization of the Christian*, 129).

47. Meyendorff, *Byzantine Theology*, 78. See also John of Damascus, who speaks of "becoming deified, in the way of participating in the divine glory and not in that of a change into the divine being" (*De fide orthodoxa*, 2.12, in *A Select Library of Nicene and Post-Nicene Fathers of the Christian Church*, series 2, vol. 9, ed. Phillip Schaff [Grand Rapids: Eerdmans, 1952]).

48. While they conceptualize the meaning of this distinction differently, that Orthodoxy upholds this distinction is not in dispute. For example, Ware writes: "The human person, when deified, remains distinct (though not separate) from God" (*The Orthodox Church*, 232).

49. Ware, *The Orthodox Church*, 68.

50. Meyendorff, *Byzantine Theology*, 2, 138.

51. Ibid., 133.

52. Williams, *The Ground of Union*, 32.

53. Ibid.

BIBLIOGRAPHY

Badcock, Gary D. *The Way of Life: A Theology of Christian Vocation*. Grand Rapids: Wm. B. Eerdmans Publishing Co., 1998.

Balas, David. "Divinization." In *Encyclopedia of Early Christianity*, edited by Everett Ferguson, 338–39. New York: Garland Publishing, 1997.

Balthasar, Hans Urs von. *The Theology of Karl Barth: Exposition and Interpretation*. Translated by Edward T. Oakes, S.J. San Francisco: Communio Books, Ignatius Press, 1992.

Barth, Karl. *The Christian Life*: *Church Dogmatics* IV/4; *Lecture Fragments*. Translated by Geoffrey Bromiley. Grand Rapids: Wm. B. Eerdmans Publishing Co., 1981.

———. *Church Dogmatics* I/1: *The Doctrine of the Word of God*. 2nd ed. Edited by G. W. Bromiley and T. F. Torrance. Translated by G. W. Bromiley. Edinburgh: T. & T. Clark, 1975.

———. *Church Dogmatics* II/1: *The Doctrine of God*. Edited by G. W. Bromiley and T. F. Torrance. Translated by T. H. L. Parker et al. Edinburgh: T. & T. Clark, 1957.

———. *Church Dogmatics* II/2: *The Doctrine of God*. Edited by G. W. Bromiley and T. F. Torrance. Translated by G. W. Bromiley, J. C. Campbell, et al. Edinburgh: T. & T. Clark, 1957.

———. *Church Dogmatics* III/1: *The Doctrine of Creation*. Edited by G. W. Bromiley and T. F. Torrance. Translated by J. W. Edwards et al. Edinburgh: T. & T. Clark, 1958.

———. *Church Dogmatics* III/2: *The Doctrine of Creation*. Edited by G. W. Bromiley and T. F. Torrance. Translated by H. Knight, G. W. Bromiley, et al. Edinburgh: T. & T. Clark, 1960.

———. *Church Dogmatics* III/4: *The Doctrine of Creation*. Edited by G. W. Bromiley and T. F. Torrance. Translated by A. T. Mackay, T. H. L. Parker, et al. Edinburgh: T. & T. Clark, 1961.

———. *Church Dogmatics* IV/1: *The Doctrine of Reconciliation*. Edited by G. W. Bromiley and T. F. Torrance. Translated by G. W. Bromiley. Edinburgh: T. & T. Clark, 1956.

———. *Church Dogmatics* IV/2: *The Doctrine of Reconciliation*. Edited by G. W. Bromiley and T. F. Torrance. Translated by G. W. Bromiley. Edinburgh: T. & T. Clark, 1958.

———. *Church Dogmatics* IV/3.2: *The Doctrine of Reconciliation*. Edited by G. W. Bromiley and T. F. Torrance. Translated by G. W. Bromiley. Edinburgh: T. & T. Clark, 1962.

———. *Church Dogmatics* IV/4: *The Doctrine of Reconciliation: Baptism as the Foundation of the Christian Life*. Edited by G. W. Bromiley and T. F. Torrance. Translated by G. W. Bromiley. Edinburgh: T. & T. Clark, 1969.

———. *Die Christliche Dogmatik im Entwurf*. Zurich: TVZ, 1982.

———. *Evangelical Theology: An Introduction*. Translated by Grover Foley. Grand Rapids: Wm. B. Eerdmans Publishing Co., 1963.

———. *Die kirkliche Dogmatik*. 4 vols. Munich: Chr. Kaiser, 1932, and Zurich: TVZ, 1938–65.

Barth, Karl, and Rudolf Bultmann. *Karl Barth–Rudolf Bultmann Letters, 1922–1966*. Edited and translated by Geoffrey Bromiley and Bernd Jaspert. Grand Rapids: Wm. B. Eerdmans Publishing Co., 1981.

Bartos, Emil. *Deification in Eastern Orthodox Theology: An Evaluation and Critique of the Theology of Dumitru Staniloae*. Exeter: Paternoster Press, 1999.

Bender, Kimlyn J. *Karl Barth's Christological Ecclesiology*. Barth Studies. Aldershot: Ashgate, 2005.

Biggar, Nigel. *The Hastening That Waits: Karl Barth's Ethics*. Oxford Studies in Theological Ethics. Oxford: Clarendon Press, 1993.

Bigger, Charles P. *Participation: A Platonic Inquiry*. Baton Rouge: Louisiana State University Press, 1968.

Bonner, Gerald. "Augustine's Conception of Deification." *Journal of Theological Studies* n.s. 37, no. 2 (1986): 369–86.

———. "Deification, Divinization." In *Augustine through the Ages: An Encyclopedia*, edited by Allan Fitzgerald, 265–66. Grand Rapids: Wm. B. Eerdmans Publishing Co., 1999.

Braaten, Carl E., and Robert W. Jenson, eds. *Union with Christ: The New Finnish Interpretation of Luther*. Grand Rapids: Wm. B. Eerdmans Publishing Co., 1998.

Busch, Eberhard. *The Great Passion: An Introduction to Karl Barth's Theology*. Translated by Geoffrey Bromiley. Edited by Darrell Guder and Judith Guder. Grand Rapids: Wm. B. Eerdmans Publishing Co., 2004.

———. *Karl Barth: His Life from Letters and Autobiographical Texts*. Translated by John Bowden. Philadelphia: Fortress Press, 1976.

Calvin, John. *Institutes of the Christian Religion*. Edited by John T. McNeill. Translated by Ford Lewis Battles. 2 vols. Library of Christian Classics. Philadelphia: Westminster Press, 1960.

Christensen, Michael. "Theosis and Sanctification: John Wesley's Reformulation of a Patristic Doctrine." *Wesleyan Theological Journal* 31, no. 2 (1996): 71–94.

Chung, Sung Wook. *Admiration & Challenge: Karl Barth's Theological Relationship with John Calvin*. New York: Peter Lang, 2002.

Clough, David. *Ethics in Crisis : Interpreting Barth's Ethics*. Barth Studies. Aldershot: Ashgate, 2005.

Collins, Paul M. *Trinitarian Theology, West and East: Karl Barth, the Cappadocian Fathers, and John Zizioulas*. Oxford: Oxford University Press, 2001.

Fiddes, Paul S. *Past Event and Present Salvation: The Christian Idea of Atonement.* London: Darton, Longman & Todd, 1989.

Gockel, Matthias. "One Word and All Is Saved: Barth and Schleiermacher on Election." PhD diss., Princeton Theological Seminary, 2002.

Gross, Jules. *The Divinization of the Christian according to the Greek Fathers.* Translated by Paul Onica. Anaheim, CA: A & C Press, 2002.

Gunton, Colin E. *The Christian Faith: An Introduction to Christian Doctrine.* Oxford: Basil Blackwell Publisher, 2002.

———. *Theology through the Theologians: Selected Essays 1972–1995.* Edinburgh: T. & T. Clark, 1996.

Gustafson, James M. *Can Ethics Be Christian?* Chicago: University of Chicago Press, 1975.

Hanson, Bradley Charles. "Hope and Participation in Christ: A Study in the Theology of Barth and Pannenberg." ThD diss., Princeton Theological Seminary, 1970.

Harnack, Adolf von. *What Is Christianity?* Translated by Thomas Bailey Saunders. Gloucester, MA: Peter Smith, 1978.

Hart, Trevor A. *Regarding Karl Barth: Essays towards a Reading of His Theology.* Exeter: Paternoster Press, 1999.

Hauerwas, Stanley. *Character and the Christian Life: A Study in Theological Ethics.* Notre Dame, IN: University of Notre Dame Press, 1997.

Hector, Kevin. "God's Triunity and Self-Determination: A Conversation with Karl Barth, Bruce McCormack and Paul Molnar." *International Journal of Systematic Theology* 7 (2005): 246–61.

Heppe, Heinrich. *Reformed Dogmatics: Set Out and Illustrated from the Sources.* Translated by G.T. Thomson. Edited by Ernst Bizer. London: Allen & Unwin, 1950.

Hunsinger, George. "Baptism and the Soteriology of Forgiveness." *International Journal of Systematic Theology* 2, no. 3 (2000): 247–69.

———. *Disruptive Grace: Studies in the Theology of Karl Barth.* Grand Rapids: Wm. B. Eerdmans Publishing Co., 2000.

———. *How to Read Karl Barth: The Shape of His Theology.* New York: Oxford University Press, 1991.

———. "A Tale of Two Simultaneities: Justification and Sanctification in Calvin and Barth." In *Conversing with Barth,* edited by Mike Higton and John C. McDowell, 68–89. Aldershot: Ashgate, 2004.

Hütter, Reinhard. "Karl Barth's 'Dialectical Catholicity': Sic et Non." *Modern Theology* 16, no. 2 (2000): 137–57.

———. *Suffering Divine Things: Theology as Church Practice.* Grand Rapids: Wm. B. Eerdmans Publishing Co., 2000.

Jenson, Robert W. *Alpha and Omega: A Study in the Theology of Karl Barth.* New York: Thomas Nelson & Sons, 1963.

———. "Theosis." *Dialog* 32, no. 2 (1993): 108–12.

———. "You Wonder Where the Spirit Went: Binitarian Tendencies in Barth's Theology." *Pro ecclesia* 2 (1993): 296–304.

John of Damascus. "De Fide Orthodoxa." In *A Select Library of Nicene and Post-Nicene Fathers of the Christian Church,* edited by Phillip Schaff. Grand Rapids: Wm. B. Eerdmans Publishing Co., 1952.

"The Joint Declaration on the Doctrine of Justification in Confessional Lutheran Perspective." Edited by The Commission of Theology and Church Relations: The Lutheran Church—Missouri Synod, 1999.

Jüngel, Eberhard. *God's Being Is in Becoming: The Trinitarian Being of God in the Theology of Karl Barth; A Paraphrase.* Translated by J. B. Webster. Edinburgh: T. & T. Clark, 2001.

———. *Justification: The Heart of the Christian Faith.* Translated by Jeffrey Cayzer. Edinburgh: T. & T. Clark, 2001.

———. *Karl Barth: A Theological Legacy.* Philadelphia: Westminster Press, 1986.

———. "Karl Barths Lehre von der Taufe." In *Barth-Studien*, 246–90. Zurich, Cologne, and Gütersloh: Benziger, 1982.

Kamppuri, Hannu T. *Dialogue between Neighbours: The Theological Conversations between the Evangelical-Lutheran Church of Finland and the Russian Orthodox Church, 1970–1986; Communiques and Theses.* Helsinki: Vammalan, 1986.

Kelsey, David H. *The Uses of Scripture in Recent Theology.* Philadelphia: Fortress Press, 1975.

Kooi, Cornelis van der. *As in a Mirror: John Calvin and Karl Barth on Knowing God; A Diptych.* Studies in the History of Christian Traditions, Vol. 120. Leiden: E. J. Brill, 2005.

Krötke, Wolf. "The Humanity of the Human Person in Karl Barth's Anthropology." In *The Cambridge Companion to Karl Barth*, edited by J. B. Webster. New York: Cambridge University Press, 2000.

Küng, Hans. *Justification: The Doctrine of Karl Barth and a Catholic Reflection.* Translated by Thomas Collins et al. Camden, NJ: Thomas Nelson & Sons, 1964.

Laats, Alar. *Doctrines of the Trinity in Eastern and Western Theologies: A Study with Special Reference to K. Barth and V. Lossky.* Frankfurt: Peter Lang, 1999.

Lossky, Vladimir. *The Mystical Theology of the Eastern Church.* Crestwood, NY: St. Vladimir's Seminary Press, 1976.

Lutheran World Federation and Roman Catholic Church. *Joint Declaration on the Doctrine of Justification.* Grand Rapids: Wm. B. Eerdmans Publishing Co., 2000.

Mangina, Joseph L. *Karl Barth on the Christian Life: The Practical Knowledge of God.* Issues in Systematic Theology, vol. 8. New York: Peter Lang, 2001.

Mannerma, Tuomo. "Theosis as a Subject of Finnish Luther Research." *Pro ecclesia* 4 (1995): 37–47.

McCormack, Bruce L. "Barths Grundsätzlicher Chalcedonismus?" *Zeitschrift für dialektische Theologie* 18 (2002): 138–73.

———. "Grace and Being: The Role of God's Gracious Election in Karl Barth's Theological Ontology." In *The Cambridge Companion to Karl Barth*, edited by J. B. Webster, 92–110. New York: Cambridge University Press, 2000.

———. "Justitia Aliena: Karl Barth in Conversation with the Evangelical Doctrine of Imputed Righteousness." In *Justification in Perspective: Historical Developments and Contemporary Challenges*, edited by Bruce McCormack, 167–96. Grand Rapids: Baker Academic, 2006.

———. *Karl Barth's Critically Realistic Dialectical Theology: Its Genesis and Development, 1909–1936.* Oxford: Clarendon Press, 1995.

———. "Seek God Where He May Be Found: A Response to Edwin Chr. van Driel." In *Scottish Journal of Theology* 60, no. 1 (2007): 62–79.

McGrath, Alister E. *Iustitia Dei: A History of the Christian Doctrine of Justification.* 2 vols. Cambridge: Cambridge University Press, 1986.

———. *The Making of Modern German Christology: From the Enlightenment to Pannenberg.* Oxford: Oxford University Press, 1986.

McKim, Donald K., ed. *The Cambridge Companion to Martin Luther.* Cambridge Companions to Religion. Cambridge: Cambridge University Press, 2003.

McLean, Stuart D. *Humanity in the Thought of Karl Barth.* Edinburgh: T. & T. Clark, 1981.

Metzger, Paul Louis. *The Word of Christ and the World of Culture: Sacred and Secular through the Theology of Karl Barth.* Grand Rapids: Wm. B. Eerdmans Publishing Co., 2003.

Meyendorff, John. *Byzantine Theology: Historical Trends and Doctrinal Themes.* 2nd ed. New York: Fordham University Press, 1983.

———. *Saint Gregory of Palamas and Orthodox Spirituality.* Translated by Adele Fiske. Crestwood, NY: St. Vladimir's Seminary Press, 1974.

Meyendorff, John, and Joseph C. McLelland, Standing Conference of Canonical Orthodox Bishops in America, and Alliance of Reformed Churches throughout the World Holding the Presbyterian System, North America Area. *The New Man: An Orthodox and Reformed Dialogue.* New Brunswick, NJ: Agora Books, 1973.

Meyendorff, John, and Robert Tobias, eds. *Salvation in Christ: A Lutheran-Orthodox Dialogue.* Minneapolis: Augsburg, 1992.

Migliore, Daniel. "Participatio Christi: The Central Theme in Barth's Doctrine of Sanctification." *Zeitschrift für dialektische Theologie* 18 (2002): 286–307.

Milbank, John, Catherine Pickstock, and Graham Ward. *Radical Orthodoxy: A New Theology.* London: Routledge & Kegan Paul, 1999.

Molnar, Paul D. *Divine Freedom and the Doctrine of the Immanent Trinity: In Dialogue with Karl Barth and Contemporary Theology.* Edinburgh: T. & T. Clark, 2002.

———. "The Trinity, Election and God's Ontological Freedom: A Response to Kevin W. Hector." *International Journal of Systematic Theology* 8 (2006): 294–306.

Mosser, Carl. "The Greatest Possible Blessing: Calvin and Deification." *Scottish Journal of Theology* 55, no. 2 (2002): 36–57.

Muller, Richard. "Directions in the Study of Barth's Christology." *Westminster Theological Journal* 48 (1986): 119–34.

Neder, Adam. "A Differentiated Fellowship of Action: Participation in Christ in Karl Barth's *Church Dogmatics*." PhD diss., Princeton Theological Seminary, 2005.

Nellas, Panayiotis. *Deification in Christ: Orthodox Perspectives on the Nature of the Human Person.* Translated by Norman Russell. Contemporary Greek Theologians, vol. 5. Crestwood, NY: St. Vladimir's Seminary Press, 1987.

O'Grady, Colm. *The Church in the Theology of Karl Barth.* Washington, DC: Corpus Books, 1968.

———. *An Introduction to the Theology of Karl Barth.* Corpus Papers. New York: Corpus Books, 1970.

Owen, John. *The Works of John Owen*. Edited by William H. Goold. 16 vols. Edinburgh: Banner of Truth Trust, 1965.

Patterson, Patrick. "Chalcedon's Apprentice: Karl Barth and the Twentieth-Century Critique of Classical Christology." *Toronto Journal of Theology* 16, no. 2 (2000): 193–216.

Price, Daniel J. *Karl Barth's Anthropology in Light of Modern Thought*. Grand Rapids: Wm. B. Eerdmans Publishing Co., 2002.

Rhee, Jung Suck. *Secularization and Sanctification: A Study of Karl Barth's Doctrine of Sanctification and Its Contextual Application to the Korean Church*. Amsterdam: VU University Press, 1995.

Richards, Jay Wesley. *The Untamed God: A Philosophical Exploration of Divine Perfection, Immutability, and Simplicity*. Downers Grove, IL: Inter-Varsity Press, 2003.

Richardson, Kurt A. *Reading Karl Barth: New Directions for North American Theology*. Grand Rapids: Baker Academic, 2004.

Roberts, R.H. "Karl Barth's Doctrine of Time: Its Nature and Implications." In *Karl Barth: Studies of His Theological Method*, edited by S. W. Sykes. New York: Oxford University Press, 1979.

Rosato, Philip J. *The Spirit as Lord: The Pneumatology of Karl Barth*. Edinburgh: T. & T. Clark, 1981.

Russell, Norman. *The Doctrine of Deification in the Greek Patristic Tradition*. Oxford Early Christian Studies. New York: Oxford University Press, 2004.

Saarinen, Risto. *Faith and Holiness: Lutheran-Orthodox Dialogue, 1959–1994*. Kirche und Konfession ; Bd. 40. Göttingen: Vandenhoeck & Ruprecht, 1997.

Schneider, Carolyn. "The Intimate Connection between Christ and Christians in Athanasius." *Scottish Journal of Theology* 58, no. 1 (2005): 1–12.

Schweitzer, Albert. *The Mysticism of Paul the Apostle*. Translated by William Montgomery. Baltimore: Johns Hopkins University Press, 1998.

Spencer, Archibald James. *Clearing a Space for Human Action: Ethical Ontology in the Theology of Karl Barth*. Issues in Systematic Theology, vol. 10. New York: Peter Lang, 2003.

Stead, Christopher. *Philosophy in Christian Antiquity*. Cambridge: Cambridge University Press, 1994.

Stubbs, David L. "Sanctification as Participation in Christ: Working through the Pauline and Kantian Legacies in Karl Barth's Theology of Sanctification." PhD diss., Duke University, 2001.

Studer, Basil. "Divinization." In *Encylopedia of the Early Church*, edited by Angelo di Berardina, 242–43. New York: Oxford University Press, 1992.

———. *Trinity and Incarnation: The Faith of the Early Church*. Translated by Matthias Westerhoff. Edited by Andrew Louth. Collegeville, MN: Liturgical Press, 1993.

Thielicke, Helmut. *Modern Faith and Thought*. Translated by Geoffrey Bromiley. Grand Rapids: Wm. B. Eerdmans Publishing Co., 1990.

Thompson, John. *Christ in Perspective: Christological Perspectives in the Theology of Karl Barth*. Grand Rapids: Wm. B. Eerdmans Publishing Co., 1978.

Torrance, Thomas Forsyth. "Karl Barth and Patristic Theology." In *Theology beyond Christendom: Essays on the Centenary of the Birth of Karl Barth May 10,*

1886, edited by John Thompson. Allison Park, PA: Pickwick Publications, 1986.

———. *Karl Barth, Biblical and Evangelical Theologian*. Edinburgh: T. & T. Clark, 1990.

———, ed. *Theological Dialogue between Orthodox and Reformed Churches*. 2 vols. Edinburgh: Scottish Academic Press, 1985.

Van Driel, Edwin Chr. "Karl Barth on the Eternal Existence of Jesus Christ." *Scottish Journal of Theology* 60, no. 1 (2007): 45–61.

Van Til, Cornelius. *Christianity and Barthianism*. Philadelphia: Presbyterian and Reformed Publishing Co., 1962.

Waldrop, Charles T. *Karl Barth's Christology: Its Basic Alexandrian Character*. Berlin: Walter de Gruyter, 1984.

Ware, Kallistos. *The Orthodox Church*. Rev. ed. London: Penguin Books, 1993.

Ware, Kallistos, and Colin Davey, eds. *Anglican-Orthodox Dialogue: The Moscow Statement Agreed by the Anglican-Orthodox Joint Doctrinal Commission, 1976; With Introductory and Supporting Material*. London: SPCK, 1977.

Webster, J. B. "Barth and Postmodern Anthropology." In *Karl Barth: A Future for Postmodern Theology?* Edited by Geoff Thompson and Christiaan Mostert. Hindmarsh: Australian Theological Forum, 2000.

———. *Barth's Ethics of Reconciliation*. Cambridge: Cambridge University Press, 1995.

———. *Barth's Moral Theology : Human Action in Barth's Thought*. Grand Rapids: Wm. B. Eerdmans Publishing Co., 1998.

Williams, A. N. *The Ground of Union: Deification in Aquinas and Palamas*. New York: Oxford University Press, 1999.

Willis, David. *Notes on the Holiness of God*. Grand Rapids: Wm. B. Eerdmans Publishing Co., 2002.

Willis, Robert E. *The Ethics of Karl Barth*. Leiden: E. J. Brill, 1971.

Wingren, Gustaf. *Theology in Conflict: Nygren, Barth, Bultmann*. Translated by Eric Wahlstrom. Philadelphia: Muhlenberg Press, 1958.

Yocum, John. *Ecclesial Mediation in Karl Barth*. Aldershot: Ashgate, 2004.

Zahrnt, Heinz. *The Question of God: Protestant Theology in the Twentieth Century*. Translated by R.A. Wilson. New York: Harcourt, Brace & World, 1969.

INDEX

actualism, 13–14, 30, 36, 38, 43, 45,
    58–62, 71, 75, 90–91, 96–97n46,
    104n25, 105–6n51, 112n14,
    112–13n21, 113n25, 114n40, 115n75
    See also Christology; history
analogy, 4–6, 9, 35, 75–76
Anselm of Canterbury, 12
anthropology. *See* human nature
Aquinas, Thomas. *See* Thomas
    Aquinas
atonement. *See* reconciliation
Augustine of Hippo, xii, 12–13, 98n75

Badcock, Gary D., 98n62, 117n103
Balthasar, Hans Urs von, 108n48
baptism, 81–84
Bender, Kimlyn, 118n1
Bernard of Clairvaux, 12
Biggar, Nigel, 102n58, 107n33
Bultmann, Rudolf, 47, 119n21

calling. *See* vocation
Calvin, John, xii, 12, 22, 37, 73, 87,
    119n27
Cartesian theology, 96n38
Christology, 5–7, 20–25, 29–39, 40–80,
    111n9, 112n14, 112–13n21,
    113nn25, 27, 33; 115–16n76,
    116nn79, 80; 116–17n82
    Alexandrian, 72–73, 116nn79, 80
    Antiochene, 72–73, 116nn79, 80
    Chalcedonian, 59, 64
    Lutheran, 57, 59, 64–65, 67, 113n33,
        116n80

Reformed, 5–7, 58–59, 64–65, 67–68,
    113n33, 116n80
christomonism, 82
church. *See* ecclesiology
command, 23–28, 36, 54, 80, 102n58,
    110n78
conformity to God. *See* correspondence
conversion, 51–56, 109n55
correspondence, 9–11, 13–14, 36, 56, 69,
    85, 94n6
covenant, 7, 16–17, 20–21, 26, 30, 31, 40,
    42–45, 47–48, 50–52, 55, 90, 97n46,
    112–13n21
covenantal ontology, 97n46
creation, 8, 20, 30

deification. *See theosis*
discipleship, 2, 51, 77, 82
divinization. *See theosis*
Docetism, 65, 105–6n51, 113n27

ecclesiology, 81, 83, 107n42, 118nn1, 2
election, 8, 15–28, 29–31, 36–39, 69, 72,
    90, 101n31, 112–13n21
eschatology, 45–47, 54–56, 85–86,
    100n22, 105–6n51
eternal life, 55
ethics, 23–28
existentialism, 10, 47, 97n50

faith, 4, 8, 9, 11, 13, 52–53, 55–57,
    97n55
Fiddes, Paul, 102n42
finitum non capax infiniti, 13, 64